MW01063167

Here Is Our Light

Humanistic Jewish Holiday and Life-Cycle Liturgy for Inspiration and Reflection

Celebrating 50 Years Of The Society For Humanistic Judaism

edited by Rabbi Miriam S. Jerris and Sheila Malcolm

Here is Our Light: Humanistic Jewish Holiday and Life-Cycle Liturgy for Inspiration and Reflection. Copyright © 2019 by the Society for Humanistic Judaism. All rights reserved. No part of this book may be used or reproduced commercially without written permission except in the case of brief quotations embodied in critical articles and reviews. See further permissions on page 8.

Published by Ben Yehuda Press
122 Ayers Court #1B
Teaneck, NJ 07666
http://www.BenYehudaPress.com
ISBN13 978-1-934730-02-7

Library of Congress Cataloging-in-Publication Data

Names: Jerris, Miriam S., editor. | Malcolm, Sheila, editor. | Society for
  Humanistic Judaism.
Title: Here is our light : humanistic Jewish holiday and life-cycle liturgy
  for inspiration and reflection ; celebrating 50 years of the Society for
  Humanistic Judaism / edited by Rabbi Miriam S. Jerris and Sheila Malcolm.
Description: Teaneck, N.J. : Ben Yehuda Press, [2019]
Identifiers: LCCN 2019015044 | ISBN 9781934730027 (pbk.)
Subjects: LCSH: Judaism--Prayers and devotions. | Fasts and feasts--Judaism.
  | Life cycle, Human--Religious aspects--Judaism. | Society for Humanistic
  Judaism.
Classification: LCC BM665 .J37 2019 | DDC 296.4/504--dc23
LC record available at https://lccn.loc.gov/2019015044

19 20 21 / 6 5 4 3 2 1   20190402

Contents

INTRODUCTION

The Society for Humanistic Judaism is 50! We honor our founding members, together with pioneering rabbis, lay leaders, and others, for their enormous accomplishments recognizing where American Jewry was headed and building a relevant and meaningful Judaism to meet them there.

Fifty years later, we know that the majority of Jews are intermarried, do not believe in the God of the Bible, and do not feel bound by Jewish law (halacha). Humanistic Judaism is the most progressive movement in Judaism, embracing full equality for women and men, women and women, men and men, for those not born Jewish and those born Jewish, and for those who choose radical and alternative lifestyles. From the beginning, we officiated at intermarriages, presided over gay and lesbian commitment ceremonies, and treated those not born Jewish as equal members of our communities. There is much to celebrate.

In 1963, Rabbi Sherwin T. Wine and a small group of prospective members founded a new Reform congregation in suburban Detroit, Michigan. Rabbi Wine recognized he could no longer preside over a worship service, even a Reform one, while remaining true to his beliefs. It also was clear that neither Wine nor the founders were interested in giving up celebrating Jewish holidays or Shabbat, or Jewish life-cycle ceremonies. They wanted to keep the baby, even though it was evident that they were interested in new bath water. Rituals and traditions bound Jews together for millennium. They were not always the same rituals, as Jews adapted to their surroundings and circumstances, but the threads of continuity were valued in each generation.

Rabbi Wine would need to lead his congregation through the steps of creating an entirely new liturgical system. He recognized the attachments individuals had to blessings over candles, wine and challah (bread) as well as the Sh'ma and Kaddish prayers, in particular. Rabbi Wine also understood the value of participating in thousands of years of Jewish tradition. How does one stay rooted and connected to our heritage, while make Jewish life vibrant, meaningful and relevant today?

Within a year, the liturgy was transformed. The Sh'ma and Kaddish and other forms of traditional prayer referencing God were dropped from the services. Rabbi Wine began to write "meditations" and "songs" all following the commitment to "say what we believe and believe what we say."

One of the first songs he wrote was called: "Where is My Light? Ayfo Ori?" His answer: "My light is in me....And in you." It continues to serve as a movement-wide anthem.

The commitment to an integrity inclusive of thought, speech, and action is what makes Humanistic Judaism distinctive. There were other Jewish philosophers and rabbis who shared a human-centered approach, but Sherwin Wine insisted that the language we used should follow and be consistent with the philosophy we articulated. When a set liturgy is no longer required, the freedom to create words of profound meaning and inspiration is one of Humanistic Judaism's most enriching possibilities for personal growth and fulfillment. The liturgy developed over time and drew on five major sources. This new liturgy provided a wellspring of compelling and beautiful things for us to say and sing.

The materials used in Humanistic Judaism were derived from the following sources:

1. Jewish tradition, without significant change;
2. Contemporary North American, Israeli, and Yiddish poetry and music, also without significant change;
3. Ancient and contemporary music, poetry, and prose adapted for consistency with Humanistic Judaism;
4. Material from the general secular culture; and
5. New creations written specifically for Humanistic Judaism.

The liturgy included in this publication fall into the fifth category: creations written by our clergy and talented members.

Corporation papers establishing the Society for Humanistic Judaism (SHJ) were filed with the State of Michigan in July of 1969. The first conference was held in a suburban Detroit hotel the first weekend of May 1970. Rabbi Sherwin Wine of the Birmingham Temple in suburban Detroit, Rabbi Daniel Friedman of Congregation Beth Or in Deerfield, Illinois, and members of the Westport (CT) Congregation for Humanistic Judaism came together for the first time to begin building the connections that formed the foundation of a movement that today includes twenty-six affiliated communities in the United States and Canada and hundreds of independent (individual) members around the globe.

What captivated early adherents to Humanistic Judaism still makes powerful and significant differences in the lives of cultural and secular Jews today. The philosophy endures. In an article entitled *Secular Humanistic Judaism*, written for MyJewishLearning.com, SHJ Executive Director Paul Golin outlines our philosophical and ethical positions and roots them in the sociological climate of today:

Many controversies in other branches of liberal Judaism are non-issues within Secular Humanistic Judaism. For example, a 1988 resolution on "Who is a Jew" accepted self-determination, stating: "A Jew is a person of Jewish descent or any person who declares himself or herself to be a Jew and who identifies with the history, ethical values, culture, civilization, community, and fate of the Jewish people." There is no required conversion process in Humanistic Judaism; instead conversion is called "adoption," as those who want to adopt Judaism are themselves adopted into the Jewish community as one might be adopted into a family.

While interfaith marriage is taboo, or at least discouraged, in some Jewish movements, it has been celebrated in Secular Humanistic Judaism for 50 years and is sometimes referred to as intercultural marriage because often one or both partners are secular in outlook. The movement maintains no ritual or congregational barriers that preference Jew over non-Jew and is fully inclusive of lesbian, gay, bisexual, transgender and queer individuals. All Secular Humanistic rabbis officiate at weddings and other lifecycle events regardless of the spouses' religion or gender.

Studies suggest a potential larger audience for Humanistic Judaism in the future. Most Jews don't believe in a God that answers personal prayers. In the seminal 2013 Pew Survey of American Jewry, only 34 percent of Jews claimed to believe "with certainty" in God's existence, compared to 69 percent of all Americans, and over 60 percent of American Jews define their heritage as ancestry and culture rather than religion. The movement's challenge remains to engage the many Jews who share its worldview but do not yet recognize the benefit of affiliating with a Jewish community.

Shortly after Rabbi Sherwin T. Wine died in a car accident at the age of 79 in 2007, I wrote an article entitled, "Lessons Learned at the Foot of Mt. Sherwin." These are the lessons and they still ring loud and true:

1. Integrity
Integrity refers to the consistency between belief, word, and action. We have already discussed this idea within the context of a non-theistic, human-centered liturgy with humanistic blessings, relevant reflections and songs that are both beautiful and true.

2. We Are Our Behavior
Observing behavior is the shortest route to discovering what people really believe. When the words individuals speak are not consistent with their behavior, behavior is most often telling the "truth."

3. Believing is Better Than Not Believing
Since the very early days of Humanistic Judaism, it has often been easier for people to describe us by what we don't believe, rather than the things we affirm. It also may be more provocative for reporters to approach us that way. Humanistic Jews believe in many things: the right to make decisions independent of a supernatural authority; the obligation to make this world a better and safer place; and that history is a human saga, to suggest a few.

4. "I Don't Know" is a Legitimate Response to a Question
If we are uncertain about what is true, the default answer is not a supernatural one. We simply may not have enough information to determine what is true. Therefore, "I don't know" is not only the most honest response, it may also be the truest response. Not knowing provides mystery and challenge. And if we've learned anything in the past few years, we have learned that #truthmatters.

5. Alphabet Soup is Delicious
As the Society for Humanistic Judaism and the movement grew, new organizations were developed. Each organization was accompanied by a set of initials. For example, SHJ is Society for Humanistic Judaism, AHR is the Association of Humanistic Rabbis, and IISHJ is the International Institute for Secular Humanistic Judaism, our movement's rabbinic-ordaining and leadership-training organization. We are continuing that tradition. In 2018 we added JFASD to the alphabet soup when we organized Jews for a Secular Democracy, a pluralistic social-justice

initiative defending the separation of church and state from a uniquely Jewish and secular perspective.

6. Human Dignity Provides Meaning of Life

Answering the question, "What is the meaning of life?" is never easy. It is also not as difficult as it seems. If human dignity is always the measure for ethical decisions, then the support and the promotion of human dignity is a strong answer to that daunting and seemingly impossible question. Human dignity is the reason that Humanistic Judaism has always openly officiated and co-officiated at marriages of Jews to those not born Jewish. It is why all members, whether Jewish or not, are treated as equal members of our organizations. Human dignity is the reason that LGBTQ individuals have always been embraced and supported. Human dignity is why prospective rabbis and leaders in our movement may date or marry someone not born Jewish. And there is no requirement that the partner convert to Judaism.

7. Hope is a Choice

When we are faced with the death of loved ones, with senseless mass shootings on a weekly basis, with mean-spirited rhetoric and lack of compassion for those suffering at home and abroad, despair and depression are normal responses. Whenever life brings despair, Rabbi Sherwin Wine's poem "Hope is a Choice" reminds us that we always have a choice in how we respond to life circumstances. Wine wrote:

> …Hope is a choice,
> never found,
> never given,
> always taken.
>
> Some wait for hope to capture them.
> They act as the prisoners of despair.
>
> Others go searching for hope.
> They find nothing but the reflection of their own anger.
>
> Hope is an act of will,
> affirming, in the presence of evil,

that good things will happen,
preferring in the face of failure, self-esteem to pity.
Optimists laugh, even in the dark
They know that
hope is a life style-
not a guarantee.

Rabbi Miriam S. Jerris, Co-Editor

Rabbi of the Society for Humanistic Judaism

January 2019

HOW TO USE THIS GUIDE

Mazel Tov! The Society for Humanistic Judaism presents this compendium to help you, your family and friends, and your community acknowledge and celebrate Jewish holidays and life-cycle events utilizing the best Humanistic Judaism liturgy created in recent years by a cadre of gifted clergy, both rabbis and madrikhim/ot (trained leaders), and talented lay leaders.

As explored in the introduction, our movement began with Rabbi Sherwin Wine a half-century ago. Following in his footsteps, and often trained by the International Institute of Secular Humanistic Judaism (IISHJ), are the Humanistic Jewish clergy who guide, instruct, inspire, and write the meaningful content you are about to explore.

Part 1 of this book lists and explains the primary Jewish holidays, beginning with weekly Shabbat and Havdalah observances, and moves through the Jewish year from Rosh Hashanah (literally Head of the Year) through Passover. Notice the shift from traditional prayers to contemporary blessings and reflections. Revel in the evocative images and literary creativity. Pick and choose text that will enhance your holiday gatherings.

Part 2 follows the stages of life and offers a variety of texts you might use as a celebrant or officiant for Baby Naming and Welcoming, B Mitzvah, Marriage and Funerals/Memorials. Note that these texts do not comprise complete ceremonies but may help you honor an individual or couple in a decidedly Humanistic Jewish way.

The **Bibliography** consists of books that afford even more explanations and complete sample services. These references, along with online sites, can help you compile your own template or unique, one-of-a-kind event.

What a gift! There truly is something here for all leaders, from seasoned clergy to start-up groups to those of you around the globe who might be called upon to lead a holiday or life-cycle service—or simply for individuals to utilize for personal reflection and inspiration. Let's share the light and advance our movement through joyous, intelligent, dignified liturgy.

Sheila Malcolm, Co-Editor

Madrikha/Professional Leader,
Beth Ami - Colorado Congregation for Humanistic Judaism
Board Member - Society for Humanistic Judaism

A NOTE ABOUT TRANSLITERATION

There are a number of acceptable styles of transliteration from Hebrew letters to English letters. In this book, we have accepted the style preferred by the author of each liturgical piece.

PERMISSIONS

All material in this book is original. Permission to use the original material in this book is granted as long as the name of author appears appended to the specific liturgical piece and no changes or adaptations are made. This material cannot be included in any document or format that will be sold. For additional permissions please contact the Society for Humanistic Judaism.

WHERE IS MY LIGHT? AYFO ORI?

For all holidays and lifecycle events

Where is my light? My light is in me.
Where is my hope? My hope is in me.
Where is my strength? My strength is in me. And in you.

AYFO ORI? ORI BI.

אֵיפֹה אוֹרִי , אוֹרִי בִּי

AYFO TIKVATI? TIKVATI BI.

אֵיפֹה תִּקְוָתִי , תִּקְוָתִי בִּי

AYFO KOHEE? KOHEE BI.

אֵיפֹה כֹּחִי , כֹּחִי בִּי

V'GAM BAKH.

וְגַם בָּךְ

Rabbi Sherwin Wine

PART ONE: JEWISH HOLIDAYS

SHABBAT

Beginning at sundown every Friday until sundown Saturday evening, Shabbat, the Jewish Sabbath, emulates the creation myth of God resting on the seventh day after forming the universe in six. For Humanistic Jews, Shabbat represents an opportunity rather than an obligation. It is a time of joy and reflection. It is a chance to rejuvenate and experience peaceful reflection at the end of a hectic workweek, and to express appreciation for the love of friends, family, and community. Shabbat rituals connect us to Jewish identity and history, and foster solidarity with the Jewish People.

Shabbat provides opportunities for both home and community celebrations. Some communities in Secular Humanistic Judaism create Shabbat liturgies based on a theme of Jewish history or humanistic philosophy, while others are based on particular Jewish works or authors. Some can even be based on the concept and history of Shabbat itself.

WELCOMING SHABBAT

B'rukhim habaim. Welcome. Shabbat Shalom.

We gather on this Shabbat as a community of believers.

We believe that Judaism is the entire experience of the Jewish people.

We believe in the value of celebrating Jewish culture and identity.

We believe that all those who choose to celebrate with us are part of our community.

We believe that being together strengthens and enhances our Humanistic Jewish experience.

May this Sabbath be a time of peace and rejuvenation.

This is a time of transition. We move from our everyday week to the experience of Shabbat.

We turn from the concerns of the outside world and become quiet and peaceful.

We, at this moment, in this time, create a community of Humanistic Jewish believers.

Let us pause and take note as we begin the journey of this Shabbat.

Rabbi Miriam Jerris

CANDLES

Radiant is the light in the world.
Radiant is the light within each person.
Radiant is the light of Shabbat.

BARUKH HAOR BAOLAM   בָּרוּךְ הָאוֹר בָּעוֹלָם
BARUKH HAOR BAADAM   בָּרוּךְ הָאוֹר בָּאָדָם
BARUKH HAOR BASHABBAT   בָּרוּךְ הָאוֹר בַּשַׁבָּת

WINE (VARIATION 1)

Blessed are those who bring forth the fruit of the vine.

B'RUCHIM BORAY P'RI HAGAFEN.

בְּרוּכִים בּוֹרְאִי פְּרִי הַגֶּפֶן

WINE (VARIATION 2)

The Rabbis and Sages of old proclaimed: We sanctify this wine.
The Rabbis and Sages of today proclaim: Blessed is the fruit of the vine.
The Shabbat makes us joyful.
The Shabbat heals us in body and in spirit.
The Shabbat enriches us.
Blessed are those who celebrate the Shabbat.

SAVRI MARANAN V'RABANAN DE ETMOL
KIDASHNU ET HA-YAYIN

SAVRI MARANAN V'RABANAN DE HA-YOM
BRUKHIM HA BORIM PRI HA GAFEN
HASHABBAT ME'SAMKHEINU

HASHABBAT ME-RAPEINU

L'GUFOTEINU U-L'NAFSHOTEINU
HASHABBAT ME-ASHREINU

B'RUKHIM HA SHOMRIM ET YOM HA SHABBAT

סָבְרִי מָרָנָן וְרַבָּנָן דְּאֶתמוֹל
קִדַּשְׁנוּ אֶת הַיַּיִן
סָבְרִי מָרָנָן וְרַבָּנָן דְּהַיּוֹם
בְּרוּכִים הַבּוֹרְאִים פְּרִי הַגֶּפֶן
הַשַּׁבָּת מְשַׂמְּחֵנוּ
הַשַּׁבָּת מְרַפֵּינוּ
לְגְפוֹתֵינוּ וּלְנַפְשׁוֹתֵינוּ
הַשַּׁבָּת מְאַשְּׁרֵינוּ
בְּרוּכִים הַשּׁוֹמְרִים אֶת יוֹם הַשַּׁבָּת

Morris Sukenik, Madrikh

BREAD/CHALLAH

Blessed are those who bring forth bread from the earth.

B'RUCHIM HA MOTZIIM LECHEM MIN HAARETZ

בְּרוּכִים הַמּוֹצְאִיים לֶחֶם מִן חָאָרֶץ

BLESSING FOR CHILDREN
(Inspired by the Hebrew Bible, Numbers 6.24-26)

I/we bless you & watch over you with my/our love,
   and I/we hope that your learning & good deeds bring you joy & long
life.
   May you help others and be an example to all,
   just as others help you and show you the paths of goodness.
   May the best within you shine forth with compassion,

and may you always lift up your face to meet others in peace.

Rabbi Binyamin Biber

BLESSING THE CHILDREN

We do not bless you. You bless us.

You bless us with your quick understanding and quicker laughter.

You bless us with your inquisitiveness that punctures our casual acceptance of the wonders of nature.

You bless us with your sense of fairness that reminds us of our own obligations to support justice.

You bless us with your natural empathy that reproaches our own cynicism.

May you always laugh as easily, stand as firm, and love as dearly as you do today.

Rabbi Judith Seid

BLESSING OVER CHILDREN – GRADUATION

In Jewish tradition we say, *v'shinantam l'vaneicha,*
And you shall teach them diligently.
And so we offer our thanks and gratitude first to the teachers.

To the students I would like to say,
Baruchim habaim b'shem shalom, baruchin hatzeitim be shem shalom.
You were a blessing on your coming in to this school. May you now be blessed as you go forth.

Our hope is that you will pursue a lifetime of learning and good deeds.
Our hope is that you will ask probing questions and think critically.
Our hope is that you will acquire wisdom and pass down your knowledge and your learning, *l'dor va dor,* from generation to generation.

In our tradition, it is a custom on Shabbat for parents to bless their children by wishing that they will emulate the virtues of legendary ancient ancestors. Our hope is that our children will discover themselves and their own unique personality.

May you be blessed in your innocence.
May you be blessed in your curiosity.
May you be blessed in your individuality.

BREAD AND BENEDICTIONS

In my mother's house
she baked breads
swollen with breaths
of yeast,
and she lit candles
saying benedictions
through lips that flickered
like the light she blessed
saying sounds
that talked in steps
sewn like stitches in a cloth.
She gave me her needle
whose swift slender shaft
went straight to my heart
where it has lodged
all these years
like a restive splinter
waiting for the flicker
of the ancient lights
to flash again
above the benedictions
told over bread
in dreams of innocence

Laurence Levine

A SHABBAT MEMORY

The white lace curtains billow
In the summer breeze
The window is open
The dusk is over
And the light of the two candles makes shadows
On the apartment wall.

How many Shabbats have there been?
Since the beginning
Can I count them on my tiny fingers?
How long ago was Jewish history?
Abraham was my grandfather
Binyamin was my father
My brother Abba is away at war.

It is so quiet on Shabbat
My mother and I are alone
The summer air and the calm breeze
Stir our memories
I begin to count all the Shabbats
How many were there in Jewish history?
My fingers are busy
I know that when one is over
There will be a new one next week.
I am always in the middle of two Shabbats
Connected and secure.

History is such a long time.
When do my Shabbats count?
How many candles will it take?
For Jews to recall my name
Can I count them on my bent fingers?

My candles are reflected
In the eyes of my warm community.
We meet to share our thoughts
Our philosophy glows within us

We touch with meaning and words.
Songs bring us together in human rhythm.
It is Shabbat again
And another will follow
We are embraced by the pattern of Shabbat.

Marilyn Rowens, Madrikha

SH'MA

Hear O Israel: Let us take up our portion in the repair of the world.

SH'MA YISRA'EL NITOL ET HELKEINU B'TIKKUN OLAM.

שְׁמַע יִשְׂרָאֵל נִיטוֹל אֶת חֶלְקֵינוּ בְּתִיקוּן עוֹלָם

Blessed is the dignity of each person, forever and ever.

BARUCH K'VOD HA'ADAM L'OLAM VA'ED.

בָּרוּךְ כְּבוֹד הָאָדָם לְעוֹלָם וָעֶד

Rabbi Jeffrey Falick

V'AHAVTA (AND YOU SHALL LOVE)

Therefore, we strive to lead loving, compassionate lives
With our heart, with our wisdom, and with our actions.
These words we inscribe in our innermost heart.
We aspire to practice them day and night,
Teaching them diligently to our children
Through our words and especially through our deeds
So that the next generations learn to revere and celebrate life.

Adapted from the traditional V'Ahavta by Jon Dickman

THE TORCHBEARERS

As one with our forebears, we affirm that
righteousness and enlightenment shall be our torch.
We shall teach these values diligently to our children
All the days of our lives.
We shall endeavor to live by these values
In the comfort of our homes
Or on cold and wind-swept roads.
Whether adversity bows our heads
Or fulfillment makes our spirits soar.
Our hands shall mete out justice to all
And our eyes shall be open to the light of truth.
We shall emblazon our paths through life
With this light as a beacon for all humanity.

Rabbi Eva Goldfinger

A REINTERPRETATION OF PSALM 104

When we peer at the sky it looks as if it were spread like a tent cloth, below it the clouds, chariot-like, moving on the wings of the wind.

Before us we find mountains that rose valleys that sank and waters that once covered the earth like a garment.

Waters rush forth in torrents; they flow between the hills giving drink to all the wild beasts while above them the birds sing among the branches.

The earth is sated, now grass can grow for grazing while humans work the land making wines that gladden the heart; bringing forth bread from the earth.

The moon and the sun mark our days and our nights.

Circadian rhythms bring forth the beasts of the forest who at night seek their prey.

When the sun rises, they return to their places of rest as humans begin their day.

There is the sea, vast and wide, with its creatures beyond number, living things great and small.

How many are the marvels that are found upon earth!

How full is the earth with life!

Rabbi Jeffrey Falick

SHABBAT READING

I am a child of wanderers in the desert, herders of sheep, seekers of water.

I am a child of slaves, toilers in the baking sun, builders of monuments to the mighty.

I am a child of warriors, defenders of their people, cruel victors over others.

I am a child of prophets, speakers of truth or power, hard fanatics of a jealous god.

I am a child of seekers after truth, scholars of ancient texts, mystics and dreamers.

I am a child of farmers and vintners, glassblowers, goldsmiths, bookbinders and tailors.

I am a child of poets and singers, laughing and hungering for wisdom and light.

I am a child of victims and martyrs. I am a child of those who fought back.

I am a child of *hassidim*, open to the mystery of the cosmos.

I am a child of the enlightenment, discovering the secrets of the universe.

I am a child of the Jewish People, heir to its riches, owner of its treasures.

Rabbi Judith Seid

JEWISH CULTURE

Jewish culture created the Jewish people. Days lived in units of seven, years marked from Autumn to Autumn, texts and contexts of language and literature—these were the building blocks of a lived experience of Judaism. This lived experience created Jewish personalities, Jewish communities, Jewish families and friends. Jewish culture created the Jewish people.

Jewish culture was created by the Jewish people. Every prayer, every poem, every story and every joke was invented or adapted from another culture by a member of the Jewish people. Every tradition and every custom began in one family, or in one community, or in one corner of the Jewish world. Jewish culture was created by the Jewish people.

Life is an exchange—we are formed by culture, and we form culture. If our identity is to be a living thing, it must always grow and change, as Jewish culture always has. We are part of a rich and varied tradition, and as every generation of Judaism has celebrated the best of its inheritance tempered by the values and ideas of its own day, so do we.

Rabbi Adam Chalom

HUMAN POWER

When human self-awareness began, we were at the mercy of forces far beyond our control. We died in infancy and in childhood, natural disaster and disease ruled our lives, and we trusted ancestral tradition more than our own discoveries and insights. It is no wonder that so many peoples in so many cultures turned to magic and mystery in hopes of turning fate a few small steps to their favor.

Today, in many ways, we have the power we once imagined our gods did. We heal the sick, bring sight to the blind, feed the hungry and comfort the afflicted. We are not perfect, but then again neither were our gods. We cannot heal all wounds and prevent all disasters, and neither did they. If lightning still strikes, we are better able to predict it and to face its consequences. The length and quality of our lives are many times greater than "in the beginning," testaments to the power of human insight and invention. Our natural world may now be understood and enjoyed rather than feared.

When your children ask you, "How did this come to pass? Why is today so much better than long ago?" you can tell them, "It was the power of people that changed the world."

Rabbi Adam Chalom

SHABBAT – SYMBOL OF PEACE

Shabbat Shalom.

When we meet each other on Shabbat, we think of shalom, peace. It's right there in the greeting.

Shabbat has always been a symbol of peace. Our ancestors called it a "taste of the world to come." The peace that they sought to create on Shabbat teased them with hopes that such calm might one day prevail throughout the world.

Perhaps it was just a fantasy. But it gave them comfort, nonetheless. We now understand that a better and more peaceful future must not be deferred to a "world to come." If we desire it, we must bring it ourselves. In our homes, our communities, our nation and the world, we possess the power to make it real.

Perhaps Shabbat can remind us of that.

Shabbat Shalom, may we all enjoy a Sabbath of Peace.

Rabbi Jeffrey Falick

A HUMANISTIC SPIRITUALITY

When our ancestors pondered the marvels of nature, they felt moved to praise. They would extol the gods to whom they ascribed responsibility for their creation. Even today there are those who contend that this is the essence of "spirituality."

Humanists understand it differently. Our spirituality is naturalistic. We celebrate the human spirit. We rejoice in the drama of life on our planet. We stand in awe before the magnificence of the universe. We recognize that appreciating these things is part of what it means to be human. To deny these feelings would be tantamount to rejecting our humanity.

There are certainly good scientific explanations for why we experience amazement at the sight of a mountain peak, sunset or newborn child. Yet knowing why we feel this way need not detract one bit from our sense of wonder.

So let us continue to burst out in songs praising the joys of life or the beauty of nature, even as we remain fully aware that our praises reach only our own ears.

Rabbi Jeffrey Falick

A SHABBAT MEDITATION
ON JUSTICE, TRUTH, AND PEACE

For generations our people spoke of their tradition as perfect and everlasting. They extolled the Torah as a "Tree of Life," filled with eternal truths to which we must hold fast in all times and ages.

Experience has schooled us in a different story. There are no precepts or wisdom that endure forever. People change. Societies mature. Needs expand. Cultures adapt. This precludes any source of ultimate righteousness that is true and altogether just.

Our messy reality demands of us an acknowledgment that righteousness and justice lie not in a book or in some mysterious realm beyond our reach. The burden of the fate of humanity is ours alone to bear.

Even the rabbis of old understood that all the Torah study in the world would never be enough to make a difference. The human condition can only improve by the work of our own hands. May we create a world based upon justice, truth and peace.

Rabbi Jeffrey Falick

TRANSCENDENCE THROUGH COMMUNITY

Humanistic Judaism is an innovative philosophy in Jewish life. Many of us were drawn to its honesty, its boldness, its openness and its creativity. The philosophy brought us to our congregation, but it is our quest for community that compels us to stay. We want to associate with others who share our vision — our view of Jewish identity. We want to share our ideas and feel the warmth of their acceptance.

The opportunity for communal acceptance is greater than what we receive from our local congregation. There are Jews outside of our area who share our Jewish outlook. They are Humanistic Jews and they celebrate their identity in ways both similar to and different from what we do in our local communities. In learning about the Society for Humanistic Judaism and the other congregations, there arises the promise of new friends, fresh ideas, different music, and diverse perspectives. This enriches us, enables us to deepen our knowledge of Humanistic Judaism and enhances our ability to celebrate our identity.

Beyond North America is the world of Secular Humanistic Judaism.

Secular Humanistic Judaism in Hebrew, Italian, French, Russian and Spanish is a mind boggling and exhilarating experience. Each country contributes their particular point of view and unique expression of our basic philosophy to our collective understanding. What we share is the passion of our viewpoint. New worlds are opened to us.

We are strengthened by this expansion of our vision. We are no longer only a local congregation, no longer only a North American Society. We are a worldwide movement. We feel the excitement that this realization affords us. We are something greater than our individual selves.

Rabbi Miriam Jerris

FOR THOSE IN NEED

In this community, where we find strength and common purpose, we turn our minds and hearts toward all those who need our love and support: those who are ill, those who suffer pain of the body or spirit, those who are lonely, those who have been wronged.

May all who suffer know that they are not alone. May they be healed quickly. May they experience a complete recovery *Refu'ah Sh'leimah* — the renewal of body and the renewal of spirit.

Rabbi Jeffrey Falick

COMPLETE HEALING (A SONG)

M'KOM HAKO'ACH B'TOCHEINU, M'KOROT HA-B'RA-CHA M'CHEVROTEINU,

מְקוֹם הַכֹּחַ בְּתוֹכֵנוּ מְקוֹרוֹת הַבְּרָכָה מֵחֲבְרוֹתֵנוּ

May those in need of healing know *refu'ah sh'leimah*, the renewal of body, the renewal of spirit and let us say: Shalom.

M'KOM HAKO'ACH B'TOCHEINU, M'KOROT HA-B'RA-CHA M'CHEVROTEINU,

מְקוֹם הַכֹּחַ בְּתוֹכֵנוּ מְקוֹרוֹת הַבְּרָכָה מֵחֲבְרוֹתֵנוּ

May the source of strength that dwells so deep within us help us find the courage to make our lives a blessing, and let us say: Shalom.

Adapted from Debbie Friedman by Rabbis Jeffrey Falick, Miriam Jerris, Adam Chalom

SHABBAT SHALOM

LITURGY FOR A SHABBAT SERVICE

(Greeting the Shabbat with Candles & Wine and including appropriate music between reflections will provide a full Shabbat experience)

Shalom – Greetings

"Shalom" is Hebrew for "Hello."

Greetings are more important than we realize. How we greet another demonstrates affection, shows concern, expresses good wishes, or even exudes anger. A smiling face usually sees one in return, and a grim nod is reciprocated. Greeting can become a ritual without meaning. Yet a genuine smile, the use of a name, a sincere "it's good to see you:" these are the beginnings of meaningful experiences.

The Jewish philosopher Martin Buber wrote that we are always in one of two relationships: I-It and I-You. When we treat people only as an 'it,' something to be greeted and forgotten, we have missed an opportunity. Genuine life is an I-You relation, when our minds and hearts are open to others. When we take the time to replace the simple "Hi" with the Hebrew "Shalom," we create a meaningful connection. It is the unexpected, the unpredictable, that shows that we care.

"Shalom" has many meanings. "Hello" can be the most powerful.

L'Hashleem – To Complete

"L'Hashleem" is the Hebrew for "To Complete."

Complete is a verb of doing: What can I complete? Sometimes we volunteer too much, believe too much in our own efficiency. Or we are too cautious, taking on only what we can complete with ease. We must stretch ourselves, and we must know how far we can stretch. Accepting a task is simple; it is completing the task that gives honor and a sense of accomplishment.

Complete is also a verb of being: What do I need to complete me? As in the story of the Garden of Eden, "It is not good for humanity to be alone." Being complete requires other people. Completion is not simply a matter of deadlines. Completion is a state of being that is reflected in what we do.

"Shalom" is impossible without a sense of wholeness, a feeling of completion. We must fulfill our obligations in order to feel fulfilled, and we are never complete without the love of others.

Sh'laymoot – Perfection

"Shlaymoot" is Hebrew for "Perfection."

Perfection is a goal that defies achievement. Human existence is always a compromise between what we desire and what we cannot avoid. Mathematics can be precise to decimal places, but how can a caress? Some look for perfection beyond our world, demanding that something be perfect if we are not. Yet do we really need one perfect way to love and to live?

We have a choice. We can strive for precise perfection, imagine the one true and satisfying existence, and be destined for disappointment. Or we can strive for human perfection in all its variety, admit that 'nobody's perfect,' and treat the adversities of life with a shrug or a laugh.

"Shlaymoot" is a goal that is failed and achieved at the same time. If we have done the best we could do, that is our perfection.

L'Shalem – To Repay

"L'Shalem" is Hebrew for "To Repay."

When we owe someone, to what can they be compared? They are like a hole in the sand: they appear entirely natural, but we know that something is missing. The sand that the hole lacks is all around us. It is our effort to replenish the hole that has not yet begun.

"L'Shalem," to pay back, is to fill that hole, to complete the other.

We have obligations owed to those who have helped us.

N'shalem – We will repay them.

We have commitments made to those who depend on us.

N'shalem – We will fulfill them.

We have a responsibility to ourselves: to constantly improve and grow.

N'shalem – We will not cheat ourselves.

We are part of a world of people who need our help.

N'shalem – We will not forget them

Others have given us the love we needed to live and to grow.

N'shalem — We will repay them with our love.
Others have given of themselves as tokens of their affection.
N'shalem — We will complete them with our love.

Yerushalayim – Jerusalem

"Yerushalayim" is Hebrew for Jerusalem, the center of Jewish hopes and fears.

Today, when "Yerushalayim" is translated as "Foundation of Peace," it is more ironic than inspiring. Yet it is adversity that produces dreams, and it was for Jerusalem that our ancestors imagined peace. We can envision a time, in our days, when Arabs and Jews might solve their disputes and learn to share the land and the city they both love. As Herzl said, "If you will it, it is no dream."

Yerushalayim may not yet be the City of Peace, but we can still dream that Shalom will triumph Next Year in Jerusalem.

Shalom – Goodbye

One can never really say "Goodbye" in Hebrew.

Shalom means goodbye and hello, peace and completion, fulfilling obligations and dreams. As we say "Goodbye," we also mean "Fare well." Shalom is not just a phrase or a state of mind or a political situation. Shalom is a connection to others and to community. Shalom is a connection to history and to the future.

As we wish each other a Shabbat Shalom, we know that this not a parting; it is an invitation to return.

Rabbi Adam Chalom

HAVDALAH

Havdalah (distinction/separation), celebrated at home or within a community, marks the end of Shabbat. It offers us an opportunity to reflect on the past week, to examine the meaningfulness of our experiences, and to use the insights gained to help us prepare for the coming week. The symbols of the Havdalah celebration – wine, spices (cinnamon and cloves, which remind us to savor the sweetness of Shabbat), and the light of the braided Havdalah candle – help us mark the distinction between Shabbat and the rest of the week.

The symbols of Havdalah have meaning for us as Humanistic Jews. The goblet overfilled with wine symbolizes joy and fulfillment, while reminding us that there is bitter within the sweet. The scent of the spices gives us a sense of renewal, recalling all that is good and beautiful and offering hope for happiness and peace in the coming week. Maimonides explained the sweet, lingering fragrance of the spices as cheering to the soul, saddened by the departure of Shabbat. The twisted candle represents the many sources of wisdom and beauty, the uniqueness of each of us, and the strength and power that comes from the blending of individuals. As we extinguish the candle in the wine goblet, we are reminded of the combination of joy and knowledge, the struggle between light and darkness, good and evil in our world.

INTRODUCING HAVDALAH

In considering the elements of the Havdalah ceremony: the light of the candle, the taste of the wine, the scent of the spices, the feel of the ritual objects in our hands, we can see how, in this most sensual of our rites, we are invited to fully embrace our human nature and to honor the age-old practice of our people of making a distinction between what is ordinary and what is special.

As the Shabbat gives way to a new week and to a new cycle of living, we too are urged once again to use our talents and our imaginations to heighten our awareness of the differences we can make in our own lives and in the lives of those around us. We have gathered this weekend as friends, as colleagues, and as people who share the same values and traditions and vision. We realize that our unique contribution to the ancient and dynamic phenomena that we know as Judaism has the great potential of being one of the prime interpreters of a meaningful user-friendly

Jewish philosophy suited to the needs and sensibilities of both a present and a future generation of both Jews and all those who espouse the ethics of humanism.

As we conclude this special day with the ceremony of Havdalah, may we begin the new week and take home with us renewed energy, joy in new-found friendships, and the excitement of knowing that through our combined efforts mighty oaks can indeed grow from small acorns, while we go, as we say in our tradition, from strength to strength.

Rabbi Frank Tamburello adapted by Rabbi Miriam Jerris for SHJ Board

BLESSING FOR THE HAVDALAH CANDLE

Blessed is the light of this place and may it shine throughout the world.

BARUKH HAOR BAMAKOM HAZEH

בָּרוּךְ הָאוֹר בַּמָּקוֹם הַזֶּה

VAY'HI OR B'KHOL HAOLAM.

וַיְהִי אוֹר בְּכָל הָעוֹלָם

Rabbi Peter Schweitzer

A CUP OF WINE

As our ancestors have done, we drink this cup of wine to mark the end of Shabbat, affirming our connection to past generations. Ancient wisdom continues to shape our lives, ancient voices are remembered and respected. Yet the flavor of the wine beckons us to the future, to shape our own story, and to sing our own songs.

Rabbi Frank Tamburello

BLESSING FOR THE WINE

"And wine shall gladden the heart." (Psalm 104:15).

May our days be filled with love, happiness, and peace.

To life!

V'YAYIN YISMAKH L'VAV EYNOSH.
L'KHAIM

וְיַיִן יְשַׂמַּח לְבַב אֱנוֹשׁ
לְחַיִּים

SPICES

Spices add depth to the ordinary, color to the black and white. Inhaling deeply, we react to the pleasing experience; the aromas of Havdalah are complex, not every day. We are an exotic people, having journeyed far in our history. Memory cannot recapture all the footsteps of our heritage, yet these swirling scents transport their richness back to our senses, re-affirming the possibilities of our lives. As we breathe in the aroma of these spices, may we be filled with the sweetness of health and the joy of fulfillment.

Rabbi Frank Tamburello

BLESSING FOR SPICES

And a pleasing fragrance enlivens the soul.

V'RAYAKH NEEKHOAKH M'KHAYEH N'FASHOTE.

וְרֵיחַ נִיחֹחַ מְחַיֶּה נְפָשׁוֹת
Rabbi Peter Schweitzer

ROSH HASHANAH

Rosh Hashanah marks the beginning of the New Year Festival and co-incides with the first day of the month of Tishri in the Hebrew calendar. The Torah refers to this festival as the "Day of the Sounding of the Shofar" (Yom Teruah) or "Day of Remembrance" (Yom HaZikaron). In Talmudic times, when the debate was settled about whether the year began in the spring around Passover or the fall, the name changed to Rosh Hashanah (Head of the Year). The Untaneh Tokef prayer begins with "On Rosh Hashanah it is written and on Yom Kippur it is sealed," linking the ten days beginning with Rosh Hashanah and ending with Yom Kippur.

Secular Humanistic Judaism recognizes Rosh Hashanah as a time for re-flection, self-judgment, renewal and new beginnings. Many Humanistic Jews gather with other like-minded individuals and participate in Humanistic versions of various New Year traditions as well as creating new opportunities for communal reflection. Most Humanistic communities sound the shofar, while many will hold a tashlikh ceremony providing opportunity for casting off the disappointments of the previous year and beginning anew.

EREV ROSH HASHANAH KIDDUSH

Tonight, we welcome the New Year. It beckons us to uncover new branches and roots. We see the symbols of the holiday set before us: a cup of wine - a tribute to our past and a blessing for our future; a round loaf of bread, a circle connecting us to our ancestors, with the whole of nature, and each other; honey and fruit, a fervent wish that our memo-ries of this coming year be sweet ones.

L'Khayim and Shana' Tova'! To a wonderful New Year!

Rabbi Frank Tamburello

ROSH HASHANAH EVENING OPENING READING

The Jewish New Year begins in darkness. We are the light.

In Leviticus, the first day of the first fall month is to be *shabbaton*, an absolute halt, and *mikra kodesh*, a sacred assembly. It is also *zikhron truah*, a memorial of shofar blowing. As the first day of a Jewish month, this assembly of the shofar always begins in the darkness of a new moon.

Neither faith nor human effort are needed for the glimmer of a new moon to grow into brilliance—the full moon shone long before humanity appeared and will outlast all of us. Yet even when the night is dark, we are not defeated. Our minds, our hands, our culture work together to bring time to eternity, light to darkness, meaning to moments. When the world is dark, as the Jewish New Year begins, we are the light.

Rabbi Adam Chalom

ROSH HASHANAH MORNING READING

Last night, a new year was born.

Like a child, a new year already has within it the seeds of the year it may become. Just as our DNA is not our fate, the past does not absolutely determine the future. As we nurture this New Year to maturity, we may yet learn from our mistakes, make wiser choices, do good and then do better.

We are the sum of our yesterdays, but we are also the potential of our tomorrows.

Rabbi Adam Chalom

RENEWAL

The universe knows no calendar. The Earth has no clock. Humanity does.

There are times when we pause our constant motion, look at the world we have built for ourselves, and wonder: What does it all mean? Is it all worth it? And can I go on? It is those times that our deepest need is renewal.

If people learned anew in every generation, we would never progress. Language, culture, and civilization exist because past generations provided experience and wisdom. Our inheritance lifts us beyond nature, beyond the cycle. Winter never learns from Autumn, and Summer knows nothing of Spring. Yet *we* have learned from our ancestors, as our children will learn from us.

We are renewed by what is timeless in human experience: family, love, ideas, and community. We renew each other with our love and support.

We renew ourselves with our commitment to core values. We are the meaning of life. We go on.

This Rosh Hashanah, we renew our commitments together.

Congregation: We renew our commitments to Justice, to Truth, and to Peace.

Rabbi Adam Chalom

STILL JERUSALEM

Give me the ears to hear the song of my fathers,
Give me the eyes to see the visions of the sages.
Give me the heart to feel the passion of the prophets;
Give me the books and the wisdom of their pages.

Let me reach to the depth of my yearning heart.
Let me create each day a brand new start
To a life of striving for the mountain's crest,
To an endless seeking that knows no rest.

The sight and sound of life's precious joy
Were known to my fathers on Sinai's sands.
Let me learn them again and add my own thoughts
To those of my people throughout all the lands.

Ideals and hopes and dreams are one.
Why stop at the moon when you can reach the sun?
Why strive for small when large can be ours?
Why grasp at weeds when we can smell the flowers?

Ideals are the stuff that fuel our todays
So we can touch tomorrow in so many ways.
Ideals are the food and drink of our souls;
Ideals are signposts that let us reach our goals.

I hear a melody from Zion,
That tells me who I am.

I change the words to know them better,
But it's still Jerusalem.

Dr. Jerald Bain, Madrikh

JEWISH, AND HUMAN TOO

"Just be a person," says one voice.
"All these borders and boundaries, these cities and ethnicities,
They are walls between people, barriers to break through,
Not positive connections of mature affection.
I had higher aspirations for you—be a person.
Affirm a common humanity;
That is your best identity."

"Who are you if not a Jew?" asks another.
"Your parents, your family, your name, your holiday
They give you away.
Your heart's feeling at the sounds of your youth,
Your language, your sentiment, betray a deeper truth.
So you doubt, question, challenge.
Challenge, shmallenge!
'Nothing is new under the sun,' we wrote.
So deny tradition a veto, or even a vote,
There's little you can do—you're a Jew."

In the old tradition, both are true.
See the world from the particular.
Be particular with a wider view.
Jewishness, humanity,
Two eyes give depth and clarity,
Capacity to see, to weep, to smile,
To emote beyond word or culture.
Each eye is beautiful, and flawed, and needed
In its own way, for its own ends.
Know who you are, and make that, transform that, live that
In a spirit of full humanity.

The simple solution:
A *mensch* is a person,
the fullest kind, to a T.
Yiddish says it most efficiently.
Being Jewish is as human
As we make it to be.

Rabbi Adam Chalom

HARMONY

One and one become one.
Voice and voice,
Note and note,
Belief and life.

If we live as we believe,
We find harmony in our humanity,
Strength in our sincerity,
Joy in our Judaism.

No one can force us to harmony
Or enforce consistency.
We choose the honest life,
A hard choice to face hard reality.

Harmony: beauty of new creation,
When elements become compound,
When yellow and blue color green,
When three notes sound chord,
When mind and heart and hand convene.

A whole, transformed beyond its parts,
A person strengthened by behavior and belief,
A community born of shared purpose,
Many voices singing one song.

One and one and one and one become one.

Rabbi Adam Chalom

A TASHLIKH MEDITATION

Community:
We arrive bearing the last year's load of leaven.
Triumphs and failures,
Missed chances,
Joys and sorrows.

At tashlikh, we cast away the staler bits;
Throw aside our regrets,
Like so many breadcrumbs
Carried off in water.

Community:
If we cast away our ills, what do we lose?
Can we learn from mistakes?
Might good turn bad?
Might bad be made good?

This tashlikh let's not cast ourselves away.
We'll keep the crumbs of our pasts,
Hold tight these few morsels -
The bread of our lives.

Rabbi Jeremy Kridel

YOM KIPPUR

Yom Kippur begins on the 10th day of the Hebrew month of Tishri. Yom Kippur is traditionally considered the final Day of Judgment that began at Rosh Hashanah. It has historically been a time to seek both human and divine forgiveness. Fasting and penitential prayer form the focus of the holiday in traditional Jewish denominations.

Kol Nidre means "all vows." It is the name given to the evening service before Yom Kippur day because of the prayer sung at the service. It allows for divine forgiveness if vows made had to be rescinded. Given that throughout history Jews were required to make promises under duress, this option was valued. The haunting melody that we know today was composed centuries ago. Toward the end of Yom Kippur, the Yizkor or memorial prayer is recited.

Humanistic Judaism observes Yom Kippur as the end of a ten-day period that includes self-judgment and asking for forgiveness from those we may have wronged—or granting forgiveness to those who have wronged us—in the past year. The Kol Nidre song is retained in Humanistic Jewish circles, however some communities have changed the words to reflect that we WILL keep the promises we have made. We have changed the name of the memorial tribute to Nizkor, which means "we shall remember" instead of "He will remember" affirming that human beings are the ones who retain the precious memories of those who have come before us.

WHAT IS KOL NIDREI?

The Kol Nidrei was never a prayer. It is a legal declaration annulling vows and oaths.

Various forms of its Aramaic text can be found in prayer books from almost 1,500 years ago. One version speaks about annulling vows made in the year that has passed. A later version nullifies vows made in the year to come. Both accounts were subject to centuries of opposition by rabbis who insisted that one could not annul vows; not retroactively and not in advance.

Some scholars believe that the popularity of the Kol Nidrei was rooted in fears that by rashness or compulsion Jews would make vows or oaths that they could never fulfill. All agree that its melody contributed to its longevity. In any case, popular sentiment prevailed. No traditionalist or reformer ever succeeded in banishing it from the evening service to which it has lent its name.

It is fruitless to tease out a contemporary Humanistic interpretation for an ancient and obsolete legal pronouncement. The real reason that we re-visit it each year is to enjoy a rare living link that connects us with Jews across space and time.

Let us now listen to this haunting refrain from the past.

Let us now experience the Kol Nidrei.

Rabbi Jeffrey Falick

KOL NIDRE

"All My Vows"
A vow:
less than contract,
more than promise.

Unenforceable, inescapable.
Unless....

Who can release me?
Are vows made to others,
or to myself?

Not for sacred honor,
Nor for soul's salvation,
Nor for fear of cosmic punishment
or reward.

The power to vow at age twelve
was the original Bat Mitzvah–
without Torah reading
or public honor.
Instead, the power to make
a binding commitment
Father could not overrule.

Unenforceable, inescapable.
Unless....

When we promise and vow,
prohibit and permit,
we decree our own laws,
self-commandments.

If we strive and fail,
we disappoint others,
and ourselves.
Yet we know that
to fail is to be human.
And punishing failure
should be to improve,
not to avenge.

Unenforceable, inescapable.
Unless....

Kol Nidre, all my vows,
all that I try and fail,
all that I want and wish,
all that I am and strive for,
all that I keep and
all that I learn to let go

to begin the new year
with new purpose.

Rabbi Adam Chalom

YOM KIPPUR DAY

FORGIVENESS

All people try and fail. The wise learn to forgive and try again.

We can be too slow to forgive others. We are long to remember injuries and short to forget assistance. Anger and memory have their place, and forgiveness does not require forgetting. We forgive by choosing not to avenge, by being open to second chances. Forgiving others brings us peace.

We can be too quick to forgive ourselves. We celebrate our successes and quickly explain away our failures. Dwelling on our shortfalls is not healthy, but neither is whitewashing them. Self-forgiveness requires honesty about the sides of ourselves we would rather not face. Forgiving ourselves brings us peace.

Let us pause for a moment of true forgiveness.

Let us forgive others, and let us forgive ourselves.

Rabbi Adam Chalom

THE HUMAN EXPERIENCE

The world we experience is larger than our values—the sun rises and sets, the tide approaches and recedes indifferent to our needs and desires. The world we experience is also smaller than our values—we could imagine a much better world, a world where good behavior is always rewarded and bad behavior always receives justice. The natural world and the physical universe have tremendous power, but no ethics. In the end, we are the ones who give meaning to life.

No one tradition, no one people owns the one true understanding of the human experience. As we mark Yom Kippur, the peak of the Jewish New Year, we know that we learn from our people and from many peoples. We support the needs and encourage the dreams of our people and many peoples. We share the human condition: finite, limited, challenging, and therefore all the more preciously beautiful.

We all live in many identities: our individuality, our humanity, our gender, our generation, our Judaism. When we celebrate our deepest selves, we honor them all.

Rabbi Adam Chalom

IN OUR HANDS

In whom can we place our belief? – ourselves.
In whom can we set the soul aglow? – ourselves.
Who has the power to assuage guilt
And to end the reason for guilt?
We do – we ourselves – we of human heart and spirit.
To whom should we give our first applause?
In whose inner being lies the power to exalt our humanness?
Let us give ourselves the first applause:
Let us reach into our inner selves
And find that which we call righteousness.
For it is not found in the heavens or beyond the mountain.
It is found here, inside our inner human depths;
It waits there for us to seek it out.
Can we give an accounting of our souls?
Do we dare – to ourselves?
What will we find
In the recesses of our mind,
In the echoes of our past?
We have the power and the choice
To narrow the abyss
Between the thought of good
And the deed of good.
Can we find the will?

Dr. Jerald Bain, Madrikh

A HUMANIST AL CHET (VERSION 1)

Humanistic Jews, like all Jews, use the High Holidays as an opportunity to reflect upon our own shortcomings and a resolution to make this coming new year better for us than the last. The Al Chet, traditionally, recitation of a laundry-list of sins, can still be a useful reminder that positive change is always available to us if we seek it.

Reader: By giving in to anger, we have cheated ourselves of peace, joy, and satisfaction with life.

Community: By giving in to envy, we have cheated ourselves of commitment and gratitude.

Reader: By giving in to jealousy, we have cheated ourselves of self-worth.

Community: By giving in to hate, we cheat ourselves of love, health, and strength of spirit.

Reader: By giving in to fear, we cheat ourselves of adventure and joyful achievement.

Community: By giving in to impatience, we cheat ourselves of the enjoyment of the fruits of our labors.

Reader: By giving in to laziness, we do not make full use of the powers we have.

Community: By giving in to worry, we cheat ourselves of serenity, confidence, and power.

Reader: By giving in to mistrust, we cheat ourselves of the security that friendships give us.

Community: By giving in to greed, we fail to appreciate our gifts and blessings.

Together: How wonderful it is to realize that the strength, the

goodness, the joy, the serenity, and the power over our lives that we seek
is already within us!

Rabbi Frank Tamburello

A HUMANISTIC AL CHEIT (VERSION 2)

Usually read responsively, with the community's sentences in italics.

Let this be our confession.
For the sin I committed against *you*.

For the sins we've committed against one another.

For indifference.
And for interference.

For minor slights.
And for outrageous affronts.

For forgetting.
And for reminding.

For ignoring.
And for pointing out.

Forgive me; pardon me - as I pardon you.

Rabbi Jeremy Kridel

READINGS FOR SECULAR SPIRITUALITY

SOMETHING BIGGER THAN US

When we gaze on distant stars
When we stand above mile-deep canyons
When we are embraced by the universe
We draw power and strength from the world around us.

When we marvel at sunsets' glory
When we hear the oceans' roar
When we are soothed by a flower's aroma
We draw imagination and creativity from nature's beauty.

When we cry at the glory of birth
When we weep at the sorrow of death
When we exalt in the joy of love
We draw hope and comfort from the lives that surround us.

Rabbi Peter Schweitzer

LIFE'S CHOICES

Life can be random, chance encounters
Life can also be captured moments and seized opportunities

Life can be mundane, repeated journeys
Life can also be precious relationships and inspiring meetings

Life can be aimless, empty transactions
Life can also be meaningful goals and purposeful deeds

Life can be lonely, disconnected survival
Life can also be shared visions and hopeful tomorrows.

Rabbi Peter Schweitzer

PLACE AND PURPOSE

I strive to live a life of self-reliance
I strive to live a life of self-confidence
I strive to live a life of personal courage.
> *If I am not for myself who will be for me?*

I depend on others as they depend on me
I nurture others as they nurture me
I draw strength from others as they draw strength from me.
> *If I am only for myself, what am I?*

Life is fleeting and I can wait or I can act
Life is fleeting and I can deliberate or I can take a step
Life is fleeing and I can choose to live or not to live
> *If not now, when?*

Rabbi Peter Schweitzer

LIVING SPIRITUAL LIVES

When we lift up the fallen
When we comfort the bereaved
When we feed the starving
When we look beyond ourselves
Then we live spiritual lives

When we let others comfort us
When we let others teach us
When we let others guide us
When we open ourselves up to others
Then we live spiritual lives

When we cherish our roots
When we treasure our heritage
When we teach our children
When we look to our past and our future
Then we live spiritual lives

Rabbi Peter Schweitzer

Yom Kippur   43

Yom Kippur Family Celebration

Welcoming family and friends

Chag sameach everyone!

The celebration of Yom Kippur is based on the idea that the opportunity to better our lives is a cause for celebration. As it is said by our forefathers (and possibly foremothers), "There were no days as happy for the Jewish people as…Yom Kippur." So in the spirit of Yom Kippur as a "Happy Day," as we prepare to celebrate Yom Kippur as a family, let us savor the meaning of the festival. And welcome our family and friends with blessings and wishes for the next year.

Here are some Jewish-secular-humanistic options for blessings on special moments like these:

Yom Kippur Family Blessing (Option 1)

Blessed are all the girls and boys in the family, and those that enter the home.

Blessed is this New Year that approaches us.

We wish for love, brotherhood, justice, and peace to dwell in our world,

And may the deeds of our hands materialize and become real.

Everyone: L'Chaim! To life!

If Not Now, When?

The tractate of Avot (our fathers) was written more than 2,000 years ago. It deals mainly with ethics and good character traits. (Today we would have probably called it the "Tractate of our Fathers and Mothers.") It tells the story of Hillel the Elder, who would recite a wise saying:

"If I am not for myself, who will be for me? But if I am only for myself, who am I? And if not now, when?"

That is to say: **If I am not for myself, for whom am I?** If I desire improvement in my life or my family's life, or even in society, who will take action and do this in my place?

The responsibility and ability to achieve my desires is in my hands.

And when I am for myself, what am I? Because when I see myself only, and act alone, or only for myself, what is it worth?

However, we all live together, with our family and society, and when it is good for all, it is good for me, too.

And if not now, then when? There is no reason to procrastinate. If you desire improvement or change, you need to act now,

Otherwise it simply will not happen.

Yom Kippur Family Blessing (Option 2)

While the family eats dessert, the senior adults bless each child in the family separately. It is recommended that the adults sit in seats of honor, with the children called to approach them one by one. Place a hand on their head, hold their hand or hug them while blessing them.

You are welcome to use this Jewish-secular-humanistic blessing. Or add your own personal blessings and wishes.

Dear_____

Son/daughter of_____

Grandson/daughter of_____

A wonderful link in the chain of generations from the days of our fore-fathers and mothers of the bible stories and until today.

We bless you today with happiness,

May it be that you should have the strength to manifest your wishes, that love, friendship, happiness, goodwill, will increase in your hearts, and that your values will always lead you wherever you go.

May your eyes look ahead with hope, your thoughts be clear and wise, good prevail in your heart, and your mouth should speak of pleasant words.

May your hands be occupied with noble and generous deeds, and your legs carry you to increase justice, peace, and brotherhood in the world.

May your life be happy, with loving family and close friends surrounding you: good men and women.

We have been blessed with your presence each day and hour, blessed with every season and year.

Happy New Year!

Rabbi Sivan Malkin Maas and Rabbi Ayala Shanee

MEMORIAL READINGS

NIZKOR

The Yizkor service is a customary part of many Jewish holidays.

The word itself is derived from the beginning lines of one of the prayers in the service, "Yizkor elohim nishmat.... —May god remember the soul of..." As Secular Humanistic Jews, it makes more sense to refer to this important part of our tradition as "Nizkor—Let us remember." Each of us must personally remember our traditions and our ancestors in our own way.

It is through our own actions that our heritage will be remembered and preserved. Through our own actions our loved ones will be remembered, and their precious memory will be preserved.

Rabbi Miriam Jerris

WE CHOOSE LIFE

Our choice is survival,
Survival draws us to its breast,
We hear the heartbeat of life
That pulses in our minds and in our hearts.
We choose life – the human impulse
To create and re-create.
We choose life to ward off
Nothingness.
Haunted by the fires of ages gone by,
We breathe the air of to-morrow.
We lunge into a misty future,
We walk upon clouds or stones
Or the strong solid earth.
Life pushes us, pulls us,
Cajoles us.
In our sadness, in our joy
We embrace it.
We create it and it creates us;
We choose life.
It is good –

Because we make it so.

Dr. Jerald Bain, Madrikh

MEMORY

The Jewish New Year ends with a moment of memory.

As Yom Kippur fades, our thoughts turn to loss. We are here for many reasons. Some have lost a loved one during the year just concluded. Others have mourned for many years. We have all lost someone, someone we loved, someone who loved us. Loss is an inescapable experience of the human condition.

We face two paths: to remember and weep for what we have lost, or to remember and smile at what remains with us. Both paths are human, both are appropriate, both are healthy, and we make space here and now for tears and for consolation. Just as our New Year celebration evolves from joy to self-reflection to mourning and then back into life, so too does the human heart change from day to day, from moment to moment.

We, who live, remember. We, who live, live on.

Rabbi Adam Chalom

YOM KIPPUR CLOSING

The day fades, the year begins.

On Rosh Hashanah, we call to the shofar, and the shofar calls to us. On Yom Kippur, we call to ourselves, and we call to each other.

The shofar's last blast has a lasting echo. It hangs in the air, fixing itself in our memory and reminding us of our promises and commitments. We will do justice. We will seek truth. We will be caring and honest and pursue our best selves. Those who hear the shofar call are committed to living better and being better.

As we leave this place to enter the Jewish New Year, let us wish each other all that is good and sweet in life.

Congregation:
On Yom Kippur, we call to ourselves. On Yom Kippur, we call to each other. T'kee-ah!

Rabbi Adam Chalom

SUKKOT

Sukkot is an eight-day fall harvest festival celebration and was the most important festival until the Jewish New Year was moved to early fall. In order to facilitate and protect the harvest, the citizens built temporary huts next to the fields, called sukkot (booths). The lulav (a date palm branch tied together with sprigs of myrtle and willow) and the etrog (a fragrant citron) became the symbols of the holiday.

Humanistic Jews retain the celebratory nature of the holiday, building our own sukkahs or joining together with other members of our community to build one together. We still wave the lulav and the etrog together in the four directions. We also may enjoy a festive meal together with family, friends, or members of our community. Sukkot is a wonderful holiday for people of all ages.

THE SHEHEKHEYANU
A BLESSING FOR SPECIAL OCCASIONS

Wondrous is the eternal unfolding of the seasons which has brought us to this joyous occasion.

SHEHEKHEYANU, V'KIY'MANU, V'HIGIYANU, LAZMAN HAZE.

שֶׁהֶחֱיָנוּ וְקִיְּמָנוּ וְהִגִּיעָנוּ לַזְּמַן הַזֶּה

SUKKOT – WHY WE CELEBRATE

The origins of Sukkot lie in the dawn of Israelite civilization. The Sukkah booth originated as a temporary harvest dwelling, permitting farmers to remain close to their crops. The Torah's authors later imagined that they housed the Israelites as they wandered the wilderness.

The Hebrew Bible claims that King Solomon dedicated the First Temple on Sukkot. It was a busy holiday in the Temple with priests sacrificing seventy bullocks over the course of the holiday. In a nod toward universalism, the bullocks were said to honor the mythological "Seventy Nations of the Earth."

The Lulav and Etrog are the second great symbol of the holiday. They are actually comprised of "Four Species." The Lulav is a palm frond accompanied by three sprigs of myrtles and two of willows. The Etrog is a citron, native to Israel and described in the Torah as "the fruit of the goodly tree." They are taken together and waved to symbolize gratitude for the harvest. Traditional Jews parade them in synagogue processions throughout the holiday.

Sukkot is also known as *Chag He-Asif* - The Festival of the Harvest. The name recalls its origins. The Rabbis of old simply called it **THE** holiday. Sukkot is the only festival mentioned in the Torah that is accompanied by a call to rejoice.

Tonight we rejoice as we celebrate Shabbat and Sukkot.

Rabbi Jeffrey Falick

THE LULAV AND ETROG

The Lulav palm frond, standing true and strong, resembles the spine of a person.

Let us stand straight with honesty and strength.

Adorning the Lulav frond are three sprigs of myrtles, shaped like eyes.

Let us behold with awe the majesty of our universe.

Two willow branches decorate it, too. They remind us of human lips.

Let us use our words for good; to teach and encourage, uplift and build.

The Etrog calls to mind the human heart, poetic source of love and tenderness.

Let us be guided by love; in all things may loving kindness light our way.

We are in possession of a harvest of honesty, strength, awe, encouragement, and loving kindness. Let us share in our bounty.

Rabbi Jeffrey Falick

SUKKOT – SEASON OF GRATITUDE, SEASON OF HOPE

Sukkot is a time of gratitude. Ancient Israelites saw their deity as the source of all good. A successful fall harvest inspired in them appreciation. It also inspired later generations and other cultures. The founders of America's Thanksgiving holiday based their celebration upon the Torah's descriptions of Sukkot.

Sukkot is a time of hope. After seven days, the holiday concludes with a special day called Sh'mini Atzeret—The Eighth Day of Assembly. Ancient Israelites not only harvested during this time, they also prepared for the winter crop. In a land with few water sources, they were highly dependent upon a good winter rainy season. Rabbis later introduced extensive prayers for rain that commenced on this holiday.

Gratitude and hope are not foreign to Secular Humanism. Though our thanks are not directed heavenward, they are heartfelt nonetheless. Being thankful and optimistic are healthy expressions of the human spirit. We can happily adapt the themes of this holiday to our own Humanistic outlook.

Rabbi Jeffrey Falick

SUKKOT – SYMBOL OF PEACE

Some traditional Jewish prayers for peace invoke the image of a "Sukkah of Peace." How can the Sukkah be an appropriate symbol of peace? After all, a Sukkah is the flimsiest of dwellings. It can barely stand up to a strong wind. Do we not desire a peace that is sturdy and everlasting?

In our day, it is difficult to imagine such a time of enduring tranquility. Unrealistic goals are usually unmet and given the state of human affairs, it is highly unlikely that people can ever completely refrain from conflict. Perhaps the best that we humans can do is to construct a peace that stands despite its weaknesses and structural instability. Though like the Sukkah it will be vulnerable to the blowing of the winds, it will invite therein all who wish to dwell in peace.

Rabbi Jeffrey Falick

HANUKKAH

The word *hanukkah* means dedication and is commonly connected to the historical myth of rededicating the Temple by a small band of Jews after overcoming the Assyrian king who sought to impose Greek culture throughout his empire. This group, led by the Maccabee family, established an independent Jewish state. Some scholars point to the winter solstice as the original holiday celebrated at this time of year. The Talmudic rabbis, however, were uncomfortable with both the nature holiday and the celebration of a dynasty that ultimately embraced Greek culture. They therefore created the myth of the oil that lasted eight days when there was only enough for one.

Hanukkah, as the holiday of lights, is very compatible with a Humanistic Jewish approach. Offering brightness during the shortest days of the year, it works especially well for the northern hemisphere and not as easily with the southern hemisphere. Playing dreidel and eating fried potato latkes provides no conflict regardless of global location. Hanukkah, in spite of its complex place in Jewish history, can always be celebrated as a holiday of freedom.

BLESSING FOR LIGHTING
THE HANUKKIAH (HANUKKAH MENORAH)

Radiant is the light in the world
Radiant is the light within each person
Radiant is the light of Hanukkah

BARUKH HAOR BAOLAM   בָּרוּךְ הָאוֹר בָּעוֹלָם

BARUKH HAOR BAADAM   בָּרוּךְ הָאוֹר בָּאָדָם

BARUKH HAOR BAHANUKKA   בָּרוּךְ הָאוֹר בַּחֲנוּכָּה

THE EIGHT LIGHTS OF HANUKKAH

The first light is the light of **REASON.**
It is the light of reason that teaches us to see the difference between right and wrong.

The second light is the light of **SELF-ESTEEM.**
It is the light of self-esteem that inspires us to believe in ourselves.

The third light is the light of **COURAGE.**
It is the light of courage that gives us the strength to stand up for our beliefs.

The fourth light is the light of **FREEDOM.**
It is the light of freedom that reminds us to take responsibility for our own lives.

The fifth light is the light of **LOVE.**
It is the light of love that enables us to care for those in need.

The sixth light is the light of **LOYALTY.**
It is the light of loyalty that helps us keep our promises to those who depend on us.

The seventh light is the light of **GENEROSITY.**
It is the light of generosity that encourages us to give even when we do not receive.

The eighth light is the light of **HOPE.**
It is the light of hope that leads us to a vision of a better world.

Marilyn Rowens, Madrikha

THE HANUKKAH STORY

Hanukkah is one of two holidays in the Jewish calendar that represents the Jewish yearning for freedom. Hanukkah comes with mythological stories about a Jewish fight for freedom. The Hanukkah story is also one of a struggle against a despotic power, and gaining freedom.

Those who come from a traditional Jewish background are probably familiar with the so-called Hanukkah Miracle story. For two years the Jews, under the leadership of Judah and his four Maccabee brothers, waged a bloody struggle against the Hellenistic Seleucid Empire. They fought for Jewish liberation and the freedom to openly practice the Jewish religion. On the 25th day of the month of Kislev in 165 BCE, when the victorious Jewish army finally entered the temple in Jerusalem they found to their dismay that the temple had been defiled by the evil Greeks and their equally evil idolatrous Jewish Hellenist allies. After a cleansing of the temple they wished to re-light the temple Menorah. Unfortunately, they discovered that there was only enough pure oil to keep the menorah lit for one day. But somehow, miraculously, the menorah remained lit for eight days, by which time enough olive oil could be produced to continue to keep it lit. Hence, the eight days of Hanukkah.

But there is also a secular tradition, with its own Hanukkah story. Those of us who come from a secular Jewish background simply celebrate the Maccabees' victory over the Seleucid army as a war for Jewish freedom. In 1948, during the State of Israel's war for its independence, Howard Fast, a secular, socialist, Jewish-American writer, wrote a novel that described the Maccabees' war as something resembling a socialist war for freedom. Fast wrote his novel in the first person, in the form of a memoir of Jonathan, the youngest and last of the Maccabee brothers. In Jonathan's memory, he and his glorious brothers led a fight for freedom. They sought to create a Jewish society that would be the antithesis of the Hellenistic world around them. It was to be a society that thrived on freedom for all and rejected the slavery that abounded in the Hellenistic world.

Unfortunately, that secular Hanukkah story is just as fictitious as the religious one. In real history, Jonathan ruled in Jerusalem as high priest for ten years, from 152 to 142 BCE. And the ancient Jews never really rejected slavery. Slavery was just as common in the Jewish world, both before and following the Maccabean revolt, as it was in the rest of the ancient world. The success of the Maccabean revolt had actually resulted in a Jewish kingdom, ruled by the descendants of Simon Maccabee, first as high priests, and then as priest-kings.

But the Hashmonean dynasty did not actually reject the surrounding Hellenistic world. In fact, its rulers actually attempted to create an interesting mix, a religiously Jewish Hellenistic kingdom. Jonathan was the last Hashmonean ruler with a purely Hebrew name. The ruler-priest that followed Jonathan was a ruthless despot named John Hyrcanus. Israeli archeologists recently uncovered a mass grave, in which over a hundred men, women, and children had been buried. Those were Pharisees who opposed the Sadducee rule of the Hashmonean priestly dynasty. And following Hyrcanus' reign, in 104 BCE, Aristoblus I, the next Hashmonean high priest, became the first to name himself king. And, like other Hellenistic rulers of the time, Aristoblus added a sobriquet to his name—he was to be called Aristoblus Filhellen, or Aristoblus the lover of everything Greek. So much for a rejection of Hellenism.

So, as Jewish Humanists, having rejected both the religious and the secular mythological stories, what Hanukkah story should we celebrate? While we do not create mythologies, the real history does not really lend itself to a humanistic celebration. Yet, we do celebrate Hanukkah. We celebrate it even knowing that the story is not historical.

In our schools, we teach our children the real history. We also teach them the mythology, but we teach it exactly as what it is, a made-up mythological story. However, along with that we teach them another truth. We tell our children that those are fictitious stories, but they represent an important fact about Jewish history—the fact of our yearning for freedom. The stories that we made up about the origin of our people are stories of our people's millennia-old hope for freedom. Those two holiday stories represent that hope, a yearning that continues throughout our history. That is indeed a cause for celebration.

Natan Fuchs

LIGHT: ENERGY, EMBLEM, AND EXPRESSION (CHANUKAH)

The theme for this evening is light: energy, emblem, and expression. Light is not only a form of energy, but one of the reasons to light lights at this dark time of year is to restore our own energy. Similarly, the energy of our community is restored with the contributions and new energies that new members bring.

Lights are an emblem – of both Shabbat and Chanukah, of tradition (many of us associate the glow of candles with our own Jewish upbringings or home celebrations), of community – as lights are often lit in the company of others, and of continuity. We light candles to signify a passing of the torch l'dor v'dor from generation to generation. We mark traditions and celebrations through the sharing of light.

Lights are also an opportunity for expression. In the Humanistic Jewish tradition, we not only offer a blessing on lights, but we also offer a dedication – a wish or an intention for each candle to represent our hopes, yearnings, or thoughts. The word Chanukah means dedication, and so as we dedicate the candles we will dedicate ourselves anew to our Jewish community, heritage, peoplehood, and our commitment to Tikkun Olam – repairing the world, and respect for all people.

...New members are a source of light to us. They provide us with light as energy, emblem, and expression. They are the new energy that continues to make Oraynu Congregation dynamic, stimulating, and fulfilling. They are the emblem of our continued success in finding a Jewish home for those who want to live culturally, meaningfully, and authentically as Humanistic Jews. And they are the expression of our hopes that our community, movement, traditions, and celebrations will continue long into the future.

Rabbi Denise Handlarski

NOW IS THE MOMENT

Now is the moment of magic, when the whole round earth turns again towards the sun.

> *The days will be longer and brighter now, even before winter settles in to chill us.*

Now is the moment of magic, when people, beaten down and broken with nothing left but misery, and candles, and their own clear voices kindle tiny lights and whisper secret music.

> *The dark universe is suddenly illuminated by the lights of the menorah, and the whole world is glad with winter singing.*

Now is the moment of magic, and now is a moment of blessing: we already possess all the gifts we need; we've already nurtured our presents.

> *Ears to hear music, eyes to behold lights, hands to build true peace on earth, and to hold each other tight in love.*

Rabbi Denise Handlarski with adaptations from Rabbi Frank Tamburello

TU BISHEVAT

Tu Bishevat is an ancient Spring fertility festival. It was celebrated as a prelude to Spring and a time for planting trees. The holiday is nature-based and not theistic so the rabbis never put much importance in it. It was revived by the birth of Zionism and the passion of the pioneers to rebuild a Jewish state by cultivating the land. The holiday became largely a project of those living outside the state to plants trees in Israel.

Today, the holiday has taken on the meaning of protecting the environment, a value that Humanistic Jews hold dear. With the development of Tu BiShevat seders, the holiday has become more interesting ritually and fun for both children and adults.

A TU BISHEVAT SEDER

What is Tu BiShevat?

Tu BiShevat (literally the 15th day of the Jewish month of Shevat) has a long history. Some scholars believe that in its most ancient form, the holiday celebrated the Near Eastern goddess Asherah, whose symbol was a tree. Asherah was a popular fertility deity and consort of the Canaanite God El. Asherahs are mentioned in the Hebrew Bible, though they are not described in detail, and were likely symbols, poles or wooden objects made from trees.

During the Temple period (until 70 CE), farmers of fruit were taxed in the form of tithes. Tu BiShevat was likely a tax collection day for fruit, whereupon it was agreed that the tax year would begin and end. Tu BiShevat become the "new year for trees." It is unknown whether other festivities accompanied the tithing. After the destruction of the Temple (70 CE), when tithing was no longer possible, little is known of how the day was recognized, except that in Ashkenazi synagogues special psalms were added to the liturgy. The idea that Tu BiShevat was something more than a simple legal requirement, that it marks the end of the heavy rain season in the land of Israel when the sap starts to rise in the trees and the earth begins it slow emergence from deep winter, may account for why the festival stayed in existence among the Jewish folk.

It was during the flourishing era of Jewish mysticism, around the 16th century, that Tu BiShevat re-emerged as a more popular and meaningful festival, first among Sephardi Jews. Mystical significance was attributed to ideas of the rebirth of the natural world in spring, and the Tu BiShevat seder, a service of ingesting symbolic foods around a festive meal, was created. The symbolic cups of wine and food are associated with the mystical worlds of creation and the human personality types. (See below). The festival gained popularity and spread throughout the Sephardi world and eventually became part of the Ashenazi custom as well.

Since the rise of Zionism and the establishment of the state of Israel in 1948, Tu BiShevat has also come to be the associated with planting trees in Israel. Like the mystical rebirth of earth celebrated in the most ancient roots of the holiday, Tu BiShevat is associated with the birth of the Jewish state today. Most recently, as awareness of the environment has become a more pressing concern for many people, Tu BiShevat has become a "Jewish Arbor Day," a day on which we recognize our ethical obligations to care for the planet and its inhabitants. The theme of a new year for trees, a time of recognizing our connection to the earth, is a most popular Tu BiShevat theme today.

All these themes—fertility, trees, rebirth and renewal, obligation to heal the world, earth-awareness and the interconnected web of life—are included in the seder, just as on Passover all the symbols have many layers of meaning created from the most ancient times to the present. Tu BiShevat is a wonderful family holiday on which to gather, sing, dance, eat and celebrate the earth and our connection to it.

Why a Seder? Aren't those just for Passover?

The word "seder" means "order" and describes the order of service for a celebration. Most often associated with Passover, a seder is a wonderful way to celebrate a holiday with family and friends at home. Some form of the holiday Tu BiShevat has been celebrated since ancient times. The idea of conducting a seder for Tu BiShevat developed during the height of Jewish mystical creativity in the 16th century. The Kabbalists, or Jewish mystics, introduced this custom, based on the Passover seder, with symbolic foods, a festive meal and important ethical lessons blended into a wondrous and joyful celebration.

What will we need for the Seder?

Table setting: The table for a Tu BiShevat seder should be set in a festive way. It is said that in the 16th century Sefat, the city of Jewish mystics in Palestine, tables were set with white cloths, scented water and candles. You might decorate the table with flowers, branches, pine cones, stones or other natural objects from your area that remind you of your connection to the earth. This is a great place to be creative and involve children. You may wish to create a Tu BiShevat seder plate, decorated for the holiday, on which to put symbolic foods.

Wine/grape juice: Four cups are drank at the Tu BiShevat seder. One white, one pink, one light red, one dark red. You can use different wines or juices, or you can mix in the following manner: the first cup is all white wine or juice. The second is white with a splash or red. The third is red with a splash of white and the fourth cup is all red. This progression marks the movement through the seasons from winter through spring to summer, the rebirth, growth and flowering of the earth and the human spirit.

Symbolic foods: Three types of foods are eaten symbolically at the seder: fruits with inedible shells, such as nuts, oranges, grapefruit, pomegranates, coconuts; fruits with inedible pits, such as dates, olives, apricots, peaches, plums/prunes; and fruits that are entirely edible, such as figs, raisins, strawberry, apple, pear, carob.

Festive Meal: You may wish to plan the seder around a festive meal, often vegetarian.

Copy of the service: Every participant should have a copy of the readings and songs you will sing. You may wish to ask people to bring a favorite reading or story on a nature theme to add to the seder. There is no wrong way to celebrate a Tu BiShevat seder, so feel free to bring in readings, music and ideas that reflect your own beliefs and ideas about the holiday. Some families plant indoor seeds or saplings on this day or include innovative ideas to involve children and friends. As with Passover, it is great to involve everyone in a "round robin" in reading the service. NOTE: If you do not know the songs that are suggested in this text, you can substitute any good sing-along song you know. The most important thing is to get everyone involved in some way.

OUTLINE OF A TU BISHEVAT SEDER

(Designed to be changed and adapted, the seder can include a candle light-
ing as well as readings and songs interspersed between the four cups of wine
and three types of fruits.)

Welcome/Explanation of Tu BiShevat Seder

The rabbis taught that there were four new year holidays. The fifteenth of Nisan, in the spring, is the new year for kings and feasts. We
call this Passover. The first of Elul, in late summer, is the new year for
animals born that year. The first of Tishri, Rosh Hashanah, is the new
year for counting years, and the fifteenth of Shevat is the new year for
tithing the fruits of trees. Today/tonight we celebrate Tu BiShevat, the
new year for trees.

The new year for trees is celebrated in the Jewish month of Shevat
because in the land of Israel much of the heavy rain season has passed
and the sap is beginning to rise in the trees. The time of ripening has not
yet begun.

Tu BiShevat is a holiday with many names. It has been called *Hamisha
Asar BiShevat*, the fifteenth of the month of Shevat. It is also called *Hag
Hailanot*, the festival of trees, and *Hag HaPeirot*, the festival of fruit. In
the Sephardi community the holiday has been called *Frutes*, the feast of
fruits, or *Rosasana dos Arbores*, the Rosh Hashanah of Trees. All these
names remind us that we have a special connection to the earth and the
very beginning of spring, even though it still feels like winter.

First Cup: White Wine/Juice – The Cup of Memory

The first cup of wine we drink is white, symbolizing the winter. As we
fill our cups we remember the beauty of winter: the quietness of a snow-
fall, the infinite variety of snowflakes, our joy in playing winter games,
the warmth of home and family, and the natural cycle of birth, growth,
death and rebirth. We remember that the wine began as a grape on the
vine, and the sun, rain and the earth that produced it. We are grateful for
all the people who tend the vine, crush the grapes, and make this wine.
We remember our ancestors and relatives who lifted their cups in cele-

bration as we lift our cups and say:

Blessed are those who create the fruit of the vine.

B'RUCHIM BORAY P'RI HAGAFEN

בְּרוּכִים בּוֹרָאִי פְּרִי הַגָּפֶן

First Fruit – Edible Inside, Inedible Outside
(almonds, pomegranates, oranges, grapefruit)

Each of the three types of fruit we eat can teach us about the world, about nature, and about ourselves. The first fruit we eat is a fruit with a hard outer shell that cannot be eaten. The shell protects the fruit inside, just as a baby is protected in the womb, and a child is protected by his/her parents. Some compare such fruits to people and the human spirit: within each of our sometimes hard shell, there is a soft, tender, or compassionate part of us beneath the shell.

Blessed are those who bring forth the fruit of the tree.

B'RUCHIM BORAY P'RI HAETZ

בְּרוּכִים בּוֹרָאִי פְּרִי הָעֵץ

Second Cup: White with a Splash of Red – Cup of Hope

The second cup of juice is white with a splash of red, or light pink. This cup is the cup representing the beginnings of spring, of hope. We know even in the coldest days of winter that spring will come and with it the rebirth of the earth. This is a time of hopeful anticipation. Even in the darkest of times our people never lost hope. We also remember to hope when times are dark, or difficult, as we lift our cups and say:

Blessed are those who create the fruit of the vine.

B'RUCHIM BORAY P'RI HAGAFEN

בְּרוּכִים בּוֹרְאֵי פְּרִי הַגֶּפֶן

Second Fruit – Edible Outside, Inedible Inside (Pit)
(dates, olives, apricots, peaches, plums/prunes)

A Jewish legend says: the date palm is filled with blessing, for every part of it can be used, every part of it is needed. We eat its fruit of dates, its branches adorn the sukkah, its fronds are used for thatching, its fibers for ropes, its webbing for sieves, its strong trunk for building. Let us celebrate that each one of us has a special role to play in making the world a better place. We are complex people and the many parts of us are needed and valued, at home and in our communities.

Blessed are those who bring forth the fruit of the tree.

B'RUCHIM BORAY P'RI HAETZ

בְּרוּכִים בּוֹרְאֵי פְּרִי הָעֵץ

Third Cup: Red with a splash of white – The Cup of Diversity

Our third cup is red with a splash of white, symbolizing spring in all its glory. This is the cup of diversity. As the earth reawakens from its winter slumber, we celebrate the variety inherent in nature. We celebrate that the world is filled with peoples of many colors and religions. Some of them are public heroes whose names and stories we know. Some of them are the quiet heroes of everyday life. We celebrate the richness of human culture.

We raise our cups to honor our ancestors and Jewish culture and all the good people throughout the world who have made our earth a better place.

Blessed are those who create the fruit of the vine.

B'RUCHIM BORAY P'RI HAGAFEN

בְּרוּכִים בּוֹרְאֵי פְּרִי הַגֶּפֶן

Third Fruit – Entirely Edible

(figs, raisins, strawberry, apple, pear, carob)

Our third fruit is one that is entirely edible, such as raisins, figs, or strawberries. Our seder teaches us about caring for the earth now and in the future. Have you heard this famous Jewish story? Once upon a time an old man was planting a fig tree by the side of the road, when a younger man happened by. He laughed at the old man and said, "Don't you realize it will take twenty years for that tree to grow and bear fruit. You will be long dead by then!" The old man replied, "When I was a small child, I ate fruit because those who came before me planted trees. Am I not obliged to do the same for the next generation?"

We eat this fruit to honor the entirety of our experience, what has come before us and what we will experience in the future. We take this moment and pause as we silently remember those who are no longer living but whose good deeds and ideas still live on in our memory and inspire us to enrich the lives of those who follow.

Blessed are those who bring forth the fruit of the tree.

B'RUCHIM BORAY P'RI HAETZ

בְּרוּכִים בּוֹרֵאי פְּרִי הָעֵץ

Fourth Cup: All red – The Cup of Hope and Strength

The fourth cup is the cup of hope and strength. Spring has blossomed into summer. This seder reminds us that the strength and power to care for ourselves, the earth and all living things is within us. We think about all our skills, talents and achievements — all that we can do to bring hope to our lives and the world.

As we raise our cups in gratitude, we dedicate ourselves to use our strength for good and bring hope to those less fortunate than ourselves.

Blessed are those who create the fruit of the vine.

B'RUCHIM BORAY P'RI HAGAFEN

בְּרוּכִים בּוֹרְאֵי פְּרִי הַגֶּפֶן

Closing Song: Where is my light?

Notes: You might wish to ask guests to bring a favorite poem or story about nature to fill in the readings. Also, you can ask the children to think of a list of the fruits that have an inedible shell, etc., as you go through the seder. If you want to simplify the seder, you can get a book like *Earth Prayers from Around the World: 365 Prayers, Poems and Invocations for Honoring the Earth* by Elizabeth Roberts and Elias Amidon and intersperse reading selections with eating the fruit and drinking the wine. Another good source is *A Choice Garden of Fruit: 200 Classic Jewish Quotes on Human Beings and the Environment* by Rabbi David E. Stein. Since there is no law regarding a Tu BiShevat seder, this is a wonderful time to let your family's creativity blossom!

Staff of the Society for Humanistic Judaism, revised by Rabbi Miriam Jerris

PURIM

Purim is also a welcoming spring festival. The Book of Esther (Megillah) does not mention Yahweh, the Hebrew god, which leads us to wonder what this holiday is really about. Scholars have analyzed the story and there is agreement that it was originally Babylonian – Mordecai represents Marduk, a Babylonian God; Esther was Ishtar, a goddess; and Haman, a Persian devil. Purim became a triumph of the Jewish people over anti-Semitism. This theme has been retained. It also became a party and carnival, probably associated with Mardi Gras and the celebration of the beginning of spring.

The reading of the Megillah is accompanied by noisemakers for Haman and cheers for Mordecai and Esther. The Megillah tell us to observe Purim in four ways: 1)reading the Megillah, 2)giving charity, 3)giving food to those who are in need, and 4) having a festive meal.

Humanistic Jews do not have to reinvent this holiday. Because the story is human-centered and its themes universal, we can participate in both the fun and the good deeds that the holiday represents.

WELCOME TO PURIM

Welcome to our Purim Celebration! As we gather together just days before Purim, on St. Patrick's Day with Mardi Gras a recent memory, we reflect on the common nature theme of these events – the anticipation of the spring season. Our human ancestors, concerned that the cycle of nature would not renew itself, participated in behavior that would encourage rebirth or fertility. Drunkenness and revelry often facilitated this behavior.

Overindulgence notwithstanding, the theme of rebirth or renewal is one that has meaning to us today. We look for ways to regenerate after the cold and weary winter months. There are many ways to accomplish this goal of rebirth metaphorically. We can plan a garden. We cannot take leave of our ordinary mundane lives and explore more enduring concerns. We can investigate ways to delve deeper into a life of meaning.

Let us use our time together this Shabbat before Purim to renew ourselves, shed our sleepy winter minds, and blossom into spring.

Rabbi Miriam Jerris

SH'LOAKH MANOT- GIVING GIFTS

Purim is a holiday about giving gifts.

In the book of Esther, it describes how the Jews began to celebrate the holiday of Purim, which they called "Yom Mordecai" - Mordecai's Day:

> *And Mordecai wrote these things, and sent letters to all the Jews who were in all the provinces of the king Ahashverosh, both near and far, to tell them they should keep the 14th day of the month of Adar, and the 15th , year by year, as days when the Jews rested from their enemies and the month which was changed for them from sadness to joy, from mourning to a holiday. Therefore, they made them days of feasting and joy, and of sending portions to their neighbors, and gifts to the poor. And the Jews agreed to do as they had begun, and as Mordecai has written to them. Esther 9:20-22*

We can give tzedakah, or charity, to the poor any day of the year. But it is also nice to remember to give nice things to our neighbors.

Rabbi Adam Chalom

SONG PARODY

Doughnut Doughnut *(to the tune of "Dona Dona")*

In wax paper, just been purchased,
Sits a snack with a sugar high.
And above it mouths are watering
Who can wait to give it a try?

Refrain
How the lips are smacking,
They smack with all their might,
Snack and snack the whole day through
And eat them up all night.
Doughnut doughnut doughnut doughnut,
Doughnut doughnut doughnut dough,
Doughnut doughnut doughnut doughnut,
Doughnut doughnut doughnut dough,

No one needs them, we all want them,
Only saints can eat only one.
Atkins, South Beach, diet, exercise:
But the mouth wants to have some fun.

Refrain

Purim comes with Hamentashen
We face doughnuts all year long.
At her finest even Esther's
Mouth would water at this song.

Refrain

Rabbi Adam Chalom

ADULT PURIM SERVICE

HOPE

Life needs hope. Without the prospect of better things daily routine would be too dismal to bear. The anticipation of pleasure and the expectation of beauty bring luster to present dullness while the vision of progress gives our feelings an upward momentum. In the gray cold of winter's landscape, we find not only the memory of January's fury, but also the promise of April's spring. Purim is the bearer of good news. It declares the imminent end nature's death and bids us prepare ourselves to greet the earth reborn.

[SONG: B'AYLE HAYADIEYIM]

POSITIVENESS

The cruelty of winter finds its human counterpart in the love of death. For the passionate bigot, death holds a strange fascination. Killing the enemy becomes the goal of life. Exterminating evil becomes his obsession. Hating villains seems preferable to loving people.

Too often we fanatically feel what we are against, but never discover what we are for. The tragedy of the legendary Haman lies in his wasted talent, in his directing his energies to negative ends. In his will to destroy others he destroyed himself, for hatred breeds only more hatred, and the lust for death, once unleashed, devours its own author.

[SONG: ZEMER LAKH]

COURAGE

The anticipation of spring is a realistic hope; it thrives on the performance of the past. The succession of seasons, in their regularity, suggests the secure potential of other things. In almost every age of vicious tyranny great men and women have risen to defy the present evil and to demand dignity of life. Like the persistent possibility of vital energy that lies beneath the white cover of winter, the boldness of bravery hidden by the security of peace reveals itself in the hour of crisis.

Mordecai is the expression of his power. Too proud to endure oppression and too selfless to flee for his safety alone, the need of the moment made him the hero. In another season and in another land he would have remained the plain peasant. But before the rage of the tyrant he awakened to his talents and found his just fame.

[SONG: OOTSOO AYTSA]

REBIRTH

As we imagine the glory of the earth revived, nature reveals herself the eternal woman. The earth is our immortal mother who, after the barrenness of winter, conceives and gives birth to the beauties of spring. The fertility of the land is no fantasy; it is manifest in the lush promise of Purim time. Mother Nature has conceived her child of hope and awaits its momentary deliverance. Like the earth goddess of ancient myth who rescues life from death of winter, Esther of Persia is the queen of life. Without her devotion and courage, the fields lie barren and despair stalks the land. Through her wailing of the Jews is turned into laughter, while the hour of massacre is transformed into a festival of exultant joy.

[SONG: OOTSOO AYTSA]

SPRING

Purim rehearses the vital cycle of the eternal seasons. Haman is wintry death who seeks to maintain the power of his cold reign through the fury of human hatred. Mordecai is the king of life, who strives to bring courage to the hearts of the oppressed. Esther is the mother of spring, whose every act is hope and whose every deed is redeemed by success of love. As for the Jews of our story, they are, like all people, rescued from passive despair by the bravery of action.

[SONG: HAG POOREEM]

MEMORIAL

The joy of Purim is the pleasure of hope. As the end of the winter is also the beginning of spring, so is the March wind the prelude to April's rain. When Haman dies, Mordecai rules, and Esther becomes the queen of queens.

[SONG: ZAYKHER]

MEGILLAH

The problem with so much religion is that it is far too solemn. Piety shuns laughter and turns stuffiness into a virtue. How delightful, then, is the spirit of Purim. The festival despises the pompous in heart and shows no mercy to those who wears the mask of propriety. If spring is coming, sad faces must be outlawed and gaiety must be the law of the land. The book of Esther can be no pious tome that we must listen to with straitlaced severity. As an ode to the season, it deserves our laughter. The villains of the story may appear too villainous and the heroes too heroic—all the better! For what we really want to do is to hiss cruel Haman loudly and to cheer good Mordecai and brave Esther with lusty hearts.

[SONG: HAG POOREEM]

[READ MEGILLAH]

Rabbi Sherwin Wine

PASSOVER

The holiday of Passover is one of the most celebrated holidays in the Jewish calendar. Some believe that's because the holiday is primarily home-based and does not require membership or involvement in a synagogue or temple, although it can. The history of Passover, like most Jewish holidays, is multi-layered. It began with the celebration of Spring, the rebirth of nature, and the birth of baby animals. The Exodus from Egypt was a later layer, which became the central and compelling story of the holiday. Although the story of the liberation of the Jews from Egypt is central in religious Judaism, remnants of the older nature holidays, both pastoral and agricultural, are easy to identify, such as the shankbone and the matzah.

Since the archaeological record is clear—there is no material evidence of the Exodus or corroborating documents of the story—Secular Humanistic Jews are left with the disturbing question: If the story isn't true, can we and do we want to continue celebrating the holiday? Although it is not difficult to identify with a story of liberation, there are many other reasons why we can and do continue celebrating Passover. Telling the entire story, both the myth and the history, only enriches our celebration of the creative imagination of our people.

FOR IMMEDIATELY AFTER THE MAGGID (STORY) OF THE HOLIDAY

We now know that the story we have just retold is the product of Israelite imagination. It does not describe actual events.

There are aspects that are somewhat disturbing. Some parts of the narrative even suggest that Pharaoh is not completely responsible for his own behavior. Just when it seems that he might relent, the Israelites' God actually "hardens his heart!"

In any case, both Pharaoh and the God of the Israelites are responsible for much torment. To our modern sensibilities, neither of them comes out looking very good.

Yet if we strip away these and other problematic elements, we are left with a theme that continues to inspire: the thirst for freedom.

How many peoples of the earth have suffered under the taskmaster's lash? How many continue to live in misery?

The slavery and redemption described in our legend may not depict actual events, but they do portray real human shortcomings. They remind us that at their worst, people exploit each other with little regard for their shared humanity.

Our legend also portrays real human heroism. It reminds us that, like Moses or the midwives, Shifra and Pu'ah, when people are at their best they are capable of performing great deeds of valor inspired by empathy and loving kindness.

The history of the Jews has frequently revealed the worst in people. As a tiny nation, Jews were vulnerable to countless cruelties. When it was possible, they fled in search of safer homes. But it was not always possible.

Their history of suffering came to an awful climax in the twentieth century when they fell victim to a horrifying genocide. Yet today, for the first time in millennia, Jewish communities are flourishing throughout the world.

Does this not call for a special responsibility?

Sadly, we do not find that adversity leads inevitably to an elevated ethic of compassion. Sometimes pain creates so much bitterness that those who were once oppressed now become the oppressors. We must make every effort to overcome this tendency.

Perhaps our Seder can help us to do just that.

Let us strive to translate its core idea into reality. Let our celebration of freedom encourage us to double and re-double our efforts to ease the lot of those who have yet to taste true freedom.

Unfortunately, there is no difficulty finding such people. They may be found in every nation of the world, including our own. They are children who go hungry each day. They are women who are enslaved to human traffickers. They are men who labor ceaselessly for inhumane wages. They are countless. They are legion.

Our path to Tikkun Olam - repair of the world - begins when we each recognize the power of our individual contributions.

No one person can change the world. To do so we must stand together. Once we begin to do our share, we will understand how what each of us does can ripple forward until it joins with the efforts of others to form great waves of change. It requires no supernatural miracles. It requires only that we respond to the best part of our humanity.

Rabbi Jeffrey Falick

FOUR QUESTIONS

We Are Polyglot

Our journey has been to many lands where we learned to ask the same questions in many different languages. No matter where we have lived the questions have travelled with us.

English

How is this night different from all other nights?

On all other nights, we eat chametz and matzah. Why on this night, only matzah?

On all other nights, we eat all vegetables. Why, on this night, maror?

On all other nights, we don't dip even once. Why on this night do we dip twice?

On all other nights, we eat either sitting upright or reclining. Why on this night do we all recline?

Hebrew

Mah nishtanah halailah hazeh mikol haleilot?

Sheb'chol haleilot anu ochlin chametz umatzah, halailah hazeh, kuloh matzah?

Sheb'chol haleilot anu ochlin sh'ar y'rakot, halailah hazeh, maror?

Sheb'chol haleilot ein anu matbilin afilu pa'am echat; halailah hazeh, sh'tei f'amim?

Sheb'chol haleilot anu ochlin bein yoshvin uvein m'subin; halailah hazeh, kulanu m'subin?

French

Pourquoi cette nuit se différencie-t-elle de toutes les autres nuits?

Toutes les nuits, nous ne sommes pas tenus de tremper même une seule fois, cette nuit nous le faisons deux fois?

Toutes les nuits, nous mangeons du 'Hametz ou de la Matzah, cette nuit, seulement de la Matzah?

Toutes les nuits, nous mangeons n'importe quel sorte de légumes, cette nuit, du Maror?

Toutes les nuits, nous mangeons assis ou accoudés, cette nuit, nous sommes tous accoudés?

The First Question in Different Languages

Arabic

Lay hazzee lay-la the-frek mayn el lay-let el okh-rhot?
Fe lay-let el okh-rhot be nak-lu aiysh wella massa.
Leh be zeht el lay-la be-nakol bess massa.

Yiddish

Farvos eez di nakht fun Peysakh andersh fun alle nekht fun a gants yor?
Alle nekht fun a gants yor essen mir khomets oder matse?
Ober di nakht fun Peysakh essen mir nor matse?

Ladino

Quanto fue demadada la noce la esta, mas ke todas las noces?
Ke en todas las noces nos komientes levdo o sesenia?
Y la noce la esta todo el sesenia?

German

Warum ist diese Nacht so ganz anders als die übrigen Nächte?
An alle anderen Nächten können wir gesäuertes und ungesäuertes essen,
In dieser nacht nur ungesäuertes?

Russian

Chem at-lee-cha-yet-sa eh-ta noche oht droo-gikh na-chey?
Vo v'seh-ya droo-gee-ya no-chee mih jeh-deem lee-bo
cho-metz lee-bo-ma-tsu
V'eh-tu noche tol-ka ma-tsu.

Rabbi Miriam Jerris,
adapted from The Liberated Haggadah *by Rabbi Peter Schweitzer*

B'RUCHA ADAMA

This blessing may be said after any or all of the symbols of Passover.

Praised is the earth in its produce and its goodness.
Praised is the earth in all its splendor.

B'RUCHA ADAMA B'FIRYA OO'V'TOOVA

בְּרוּכָה אָדָמָה בְּפִרְיָה וּבְטוּבָה

B'RUCHA ADAMA B'CHOL OD TIFARTA.

בְּרוּכָה אָדָמָה בְּכָל עוֹד תִּפְאַרְתָּה

Rabbis Peter Schweitzer and Sherwin Wine

MATZAH

Matzah – Why do we eat Matzah?

Matzah is the bread of freedom. Legend has it that when our ancestors fled Egypt they moved so quickly that the bread they baked did not have time to rise. Scholars tell us that in ancient Israel that bread was baked from the unfermented grain of the spring harvest to celebrate the newness of the reborn earth. Matzah is the bread of dignity, preferring liberty to luxury, avoiding pretense. It is the bread of life, rejecting the cold slavery of winter, affirming the warm vitality of spring.

Rabbi Sherwin Wine

MAROR

Maror – Why do we eat maror tonight?

To remind us of the bitterness of our slavery and the gift of our freedom that we too often take for granted.

And to remind us that our ancestors ate bitter herbs at the time of the spring festival. The sharpness of the taste reawakened their senses and made them feel as one with the revival of nature.

And to teach us, too, that not all know the taste of freedom. Let us also remember the embittered lives of all those in the world who remain in bondage, physically, mentally, and continue to suffer without relief.

Rabbi Peter Schweitzer

HAROSET

Haroset – Why do we eat haroset?

Haroset is a condiment of apples, nuts, cinnamon, and wine. It looks like the bricks, which, according to tradition, our ancestors made for the king of Egypt. Many see it as a sign of the bondage our ancestors refused to accept when they fled Egypt. It is also a sign of the joy of freedom. Liberty is not only the pain of struggle and risky decision. It is also the sweetness of useful work, good friends, and satisfying leisure. Just as the parsley is dipped in salt water to sharpen its flavor, so do we dip the unleavened bread or the bitter herb into the haroset to sweeten our taste. In this season of life, we must remember the goodness of life.

Rabbi Sherwin Wine

BAYTSA

Baytsa – Why do we eat baytsa tonight?

To remind us of the special Festival Offering by which the priests, in Temple days, expressed their gratitude for the well-being of the people. And to remind us that eggs are the symbol of life, or birth and rebirth. As all around us nature dances with new life so may this season stir within us new strength, new hope, and new joy.

And to teach us, too, that the egg, which becomes harder and tougher when heat is applied, symbolizes the toughness of the Jewish people to endure and persevere despite our suffering.

Rabbi Peter Schweitzer

A HISTORICAL PERSPECTIVE ON THE EXODUS

When earlier we recalled the story of the Exodus, we acknowledged it as a work of fiction. Yet only one hundred years ago, most scholars still believed that the tale was true in many of its details.

Then they started digging ... literally ... with shovels and pails. It eventually became clear that the story we had told ourselves for millennia did not take place. There had been no mass flight from Egypt, no conquest of the land of Israel, otherwise known as Canaan. The Israelites were natives of the land; they were Canaanites themselves!

So how did the story come to be?

In the late second millennium B.C.E., Egypt dominated Canaan. The pharaohs demanded regular tribute from vassal kings who in turn exploited their own peasant populations.

According to some scholars, in the thirteenth century B.C.E. the region experienced significant upheavals and power shifts. Taking advantage of these changes, many peasants rebelled, throwing off the yoke of their vassal kings. Archeological remains reveal that some fled to and cleared Israel's central highlands, where tribes and towns began to form. In a long, complicated and gradual process they became known as the Israelites. Did this contribute to inspiring our story?

If so, the Exodus tale may have served as an allegory about liberation from Egypt's ongoing domination and exploitation of Canaan's populace. The narrative may also reflect other ancient regional instabilities. Famines and droughts provoked repeated migrations. The Torah's stories about Abraham and Sara's journey to Canaan and their grandchildren's descent to Egypt may disclose memories of these population shifts.

Other historians suggest an alternative possibility. They propose that the Exodus story was influenced by the experience of one tribe, the Levites that may have come to Israel from Egypt. Many Levite names, including Moses and Aaron, are Egyptian in origin. The Levites were cultic experts and possessed no territory. Were they the outsiders who circulated the original Exodus tale?

The details are buried in history, but history gives wings to legends and legends yield heroes like Moses. Over hundreds of years, our story emerged with its account of one great man, dedicated to justice and to the liberation of his people. He challenged Pharaoh and led the Israelites to freedom. For millennia he has inspired many others who have been downtrodden or enslaved to bring about their own deliverance. And that's why we told it tonight!

Rabbi Jeffrey Falick

CUP OF MIRIAM

The legends of our Rabbinic sages teach us that a miraculous well of healing waters accompanied the children of Israel throughout their journey in the desert, providing them with water. This well was given to Miriam, the prophetess, to honor her bravery and devotion to the Jewish people. According to the legend, both Miriam and her well provided comfort and gave our forbearers the faith and confidence to overcome the hardships of the Exodus. We fill Miriam's cup with water to honor her contribution to the Jewish people. Like Miriam, Jewish women in all generations have been essential for the continuity of our people. Women passed down songs and stories, rituals and recipes, from mother to daughter, from generation to generation. Let us each fill the cup of Miriam with water from our own glasses, so that our children may continue to draw from the strength and wisdom of our heritage.

We place Miriam's cup on our Seder table to honor the important and often unrecognized role of Jewish women in our tradition and history, to tell their stories that have been too sparingly told.

Rabbi Miriam Jerris

AFIKOMEN

Like many customs in the Jewish tradition, the origin of the afikomen has little to do with the current practice. The distinctly Greek word has the connotation of "gadding around on revels." The Talmud says that "men must not leave the pascal meal *epikomin.*" The phrase became misunderstood until it meant that the meal could not be concluded until the afikomen, thereby taking on the meaning of dessert.

The afikomen, one half of the matzah that was broken at the beginning of the Seder, is traditionally hidden, and searched for by the children present at the Seder. The idea of searching gives rise to the metaphor that we too, treasure the search for truth and freedom in this world. Before we share in the afikomen, let us reconnect the two halves of the matzah, and see this as a sign that what is broken off is not really lost to us, as long as we continue to search for it.

Sharing the afikomen as the last taste of supper reaffirms our pleasure in "breaking bread" together.

Rabbi Miriam Jerris

BIBLIOGRAPHY: HOLIDAYS

Bloom, Valerie Toizer. *Celebrating the Jewish Holidays: Life-Affirming Secular and Spiritual Observances.* San Bernardino, CA: Self-published, 2014.

Falk, Marcia. *The Book of Blessings.* Boston: Beacon Press, 1996.

Levine, Herbert. *Words for Blessing the World: Poems in Hebrew and English.* Teaneck, NJ: Ben Yehuda Press, 2017.

Muraskin, Bennett, Judith Seid and Lawrence Schofer. *Celebrating Jewish Holidays: An Introduction for Secular Jewish Families and Their Communities.* Southfield, MI: 2002.

Piercy, Marge. *The Art of Blessing the Day: Poems with a Jewish Theme.* New York: 2000.

Piercy, Marge. *Pesach for the Rest of Us: Making the Passover Seder Your Own.* New York: Schoken Books, 2007.

Roberts, Elizabeth and Elias Amidon. *Life Prayers: 365 Prayers, Blessings and Affirmations to Celebrate the Human Journey.* New York: HarperCollins, 1991.

Seid, Judith. *God-Optional Judaism: Alternatives for Cultural Jews Who Love Their History, Heritage, and Community.* New York: Kensington Publishing, 2001.

Society for Humanistic Judaism, "The High Holidays," *Humanistic Judaism,* (Spring 1986)

Society for Humanistic Judaism, "Sukkot," *Humanistic Judaism,* (Summer 1990)

Society for Humanistic Judaism, "A Hanukka Manual," *Humanistic Judaism.*

Society for Humanistic Judaism, "Tu Bi-Shevat: The Jewish Earth Day," *Humanistic Judaism,* (Winter 1993)

Society for Humanistic Judaism, "Purim," *Humanistic Judaism,* (Winter 1992)

Society for Humanistic Judaism, "A Passover Manual," *Humanistic Judaism.*

Society for Humanistic Judaism, "Shavuot: Discovering Our Literature," *Humanistic Judaism,* (Spring 1995)

Shulevitz, Judith. *The Sabbath World: Glimpses of a Different Order of Time.* New York: Random House, 2010.

Wine, Sherwin T. *Celebration: A Ceremonial and Philosophic Guide for Humanists and Humanistic Jews.* Buffalo, New York: Prometheus Books, 1988.

PART TWO: LIFE CYCLES

BIRTH CELEBRATIONS

AND BABY NAMINGS

In Biblical times, the birth of a male child was more important than the birth of a female in Jewish ritual and tradition. Given the status of women in this era, it is not surprising. Both Brit Mila or Bris and Pidyon HaBen are described in the Biblical text. At the Brit Milah ceremony baby boys are given a Hebrew name. Girls are often named in the synagogue about a month following their birth. In Orthodox and Conservative Judaism, a child is Jewish if the mother was born Jewish or converted to Judaism through their denomination. Reform and Reconstructionist Jews recognize that children born of only a Jewish father are also Jewish.

Secular Humanistic Judaism has a different approach to the birth of a child. Jewish identity is a function of self-identification. If the parents are choosing to identify their child with the Jewish people, we will acknowledge and celebrate that identity with a Birth Celebration and Naming. For us, in these times, a child is equally celebrated, no matter the gender. All children are treated equally in these ceremonies. Among intermarried families, there are no additional requirements to celebrate the child regardless of which parent is Jewish by birth or conversion. Decisions about Brit Mila are personal decisions to be made by the parents. Some Humanistic rabbis and leaders will participate in a joint Brit Milah and Birth Celebration; others will not.

PRIOR TO BIRTH: MOTHERWELL CEREMONY

A Motherwell ceremony comes from the Navajo tradition. Rather than a baby shower, a pregnant person is cared for by their circle of friends (often a group of women). This ceremony draws on the tradition of the mikvah, the ritual bath. Some elements of this can be used for a private mikvah ceremony as well (there are some progressive mikvahs one can visit or some people find a flowing body of water and take a DIY approach).

Pregnancy and birth are hugely transformative experiences. This ceremony is designed to help mark the transformations and transitions with intention, with support, and with meaning.

Welcome everyone! This ceremony is about endings and new beginnings. We are the women who are most important to _____. It's my pleasure to welcome you as we celebrate _____ and her special moment, and our interwoven experiences as the women in her life.

...Before, during, or after birth, water is used for a mother's comfort and also connection to her ancestral past. Her baby is immersed, and then so is she. The story of the Jewish people, born out of Exodus (a story which starts with a birth, brave midwives, and a mother's will to protect her child), is one of rebirth and redemption. We find both in the symbolic waters.

...Let us allow ourselves to be fully present this morning (afternoon/ evening), thrilled to be alive and to be together.

The mikvah is an aspect of traditional Judaism that reflects the sexism of the tradition. Women are commanded to enter the mikvah after menstruation because they need to be "purified." This has to do with revulsion for the female body and also the linking a lack of conception with death.

Today we take the traditions and transform them. The mikvah is a symbol of transformation, and we transform its symbolism. As these waters move, they move our interpretation of mikvah as a symbol of the need to purify the body to a need to purify the heart, mind, and spirit.

Sometimes the tradition leads to unforeseen consequences. From the sexist tradition grew female-only spaces. The mikvah is a women-identified space and we celebrate that space together, today.

...To take back the waters means to see mikvah as a wholly female experience.

Just as Miriam's well gave water to the Israelites, so too will the mikveh give strength back to Jewish women. Water is the symbol of birth — and now it can be a symbol of rebirth. Immersion and submersion each have their own particular meanings. Today we wish for_____ to immerse herself in our love. We want her to feel immersed in the joy of her pregnancy and birth. We all immerse ourselves in celebration along with her. Submersion can also have multiple meanings...

...Immersion in water can symbolize birth and rebirth. It is about connection to the natural world and to those held within its depths. It can also be about release. As those of us who choose to go in the water immerse ourselves, it is an opportunity to consider what we'd like to let go of – to let float away. And as we emerge we can find new completeness that centres around new positivity.

Final Mikvah blessing:
May I step into a life filled with continued wisdom and deeds of kindness. May I step forward into a life filled with the blessing of new beginnings. May I prove to be a loving and joyful mother. I am grateful to the women in my life who are with me in this journey. May we all be blessed in going out into a life of fulfillment and peace.

Rabbi Denise Handlarski

OPENING BLESSING FOR BIRTH CELEBRATION OR BABY NAMING

Love
We come together in love.
We come together in the love of family and friends.
We come together in the love that new life needs.

Rabbi Sherwin Wine

WELCOME CHILD BIRTH OR ADOPTION

B'rukhim ha-ba`im /בְּרוּכִים הַבָּאִים. Welcome.

____(Parent and sibling name/s)____ invited us to come together to celebrate ____(child)__'s birth/adoption and naming, and, in our various ways, to pledge to them/him/her (parent/s) our support for their parenting and family, and for __(child)'s__ growth.

We have gathered here today to welcome ____(child's name with or without middle name/s and surname/s)____ into this community of loving family and friends, and into this world full of diverse peoples and possibilities.

Being here reminds us that in every child's birth we encounter the eternal rebirth of life's meaning, beauty, and wonder. Infants help us to encounter human vulnerability and interdependence, and to sense our roles in the cycles of life's renewal. Babies make us aware that the world surrounds us with vast horizons. Children awaken us to see again the world with new eyes. They help us remember that we can all explore and grow, that we can all fall down and stand up again, and that we all need continuing love and learning.

Indeed, love and sharing are the foundations of our human covenant for a better world.

Loving and helping one another, we stretch beyond selfishness toward transcendence: giving to others helps not only them, but ourselves as well.

The more love and support we give, the more we are likely to receive; the more we receive, the more likely we are to give. The mutual gift of loving words and deeds — in Hebrew, called *g'milut hasadim* / גְּמִילוּת חֲסָדִים — is the greatest offering that we can bestow upon each other.

Thus, let us all give _____(child's name)_____ the bounty of our love, so that s/he will feel the heights of its joy and the depths of its pathos, so that s/he will live a life overflowing with love with all its liberating and healing power.

Mindful of the preciousness and potentials of life, we gather here to-day to expand the human covenant for a better world.

For the sake of generations living and those to come, may our words and deeds foster improvement of the world, *tiqqun ha-olam* / תִּקּוּן הָעוֹלָם.

For _____(child)_____'s sake, may we all do our best in helping her/him to grow and learn, to explore and feel secure, to play and work, to love and feel loved.

May we help her/him to face challenges with confidence, creativity, and compassion, to win and lose with grace and good-humor, and, in her/his own time, to develop the fullness of her/his humanity - in Yid-dish, her/his *mentshlekhkeit* / מענטשלעכקייט - as s/he learns how to be a decent and mature person.

Rabbi Binyamin Biber

BABY NAMING REFLECTIONS

CREATIVITY

Love is an expression of our strength. To nurture another human being with the gift of our time and our talents is to affirm our own power to create. True love is never self-sacrifice. It is the overflow of vitality which allows the force of life to pass from one to another.

To love a child is to love life. To nurture an infant is to express hope. Children do not steal our strength. They allow us to go beyond ourselves to discover the power of our own creative talents in their success. To be a father or a mother is more than a profession. It is the fulfillment of one our deepest needs – our need to touch the future and to make it live.

You have touched the future with your own creative power. You have brought a new child into the world. You are parents by choice and desire. May your newborn son/daughter bring you more life through his/her life. May s/he always enable you to reach out beyond yourselves to love and to nurture. May the name you have given him/her, _____, always be an affirmation of life.

Rabbi Sherwin Wine

FAMILY

Life offers the gift of many blessings. None is more precious than the love of family. In the strength and compassion of parents, in the loyalty of brothers and sisters, in mutual devotion of husband and wife, we find the security of our love. Even the sweet affection of children brings its special charm and warms our attachment to life. The landscape of our days is peopled by the secure presence of open hearts that exact no price for the gift of themselves.

Your child is now an intimate part of your family circle. S/he needs your strength. S/he needs your compassion. S/he needs your nurturing love. In turn, s/he will give you the warmth of new life. May the name s/he now bears, _____, be a reminder of his/her family connection. May it always be a sign of his/her firm attachment to life.

Rabbi Sherwin Wine

LOVE

Love is not an abstraction. It is a passion of the heart, an expression of the body, deeply rooted in life and human existence. Our first experience of love starts when we are helpless infants, when we are completely dependent on the care and attention of our mother and father. They hold us and feed us and make sure that we are warm. They respond to our needs and do for us what we cannot do for ourselves. They make us feel safe and secure. Above all, they give us a sense of specialness and significance. Without their love, we would not come to love ourselves and to find our self-esteem. Nor would we ever learn to love others.

Your new son/daughter will learn love from you. S/he will learn to love herself/himself because you love her/him. S/he will learn to love others because you have shown him/her how it is possible to reach out to another human being and to embrace him/her with caring warmth. Right now you are teaching him/her the most important lesson of life, the lesson of love.

May this experience fill his/her life with deep satisfaction. May the name s/he bears, _____, unite him/her with all his/her family roots, the hopes of the past and the promise of his/her future. May the love s/he now receives be an intimation of the love s/he will in turn give to others as s/he assumes the responsibilities of his/her own life.

Rabbi Sherwin Wine

BONDING

Newborn infants have a way of changing the lives of those who love them. They are so warm, soft, and cuddly that it is very hard to resist picking them up and holding them. They are so charmingly naïve, fresh, and curious that it is difficult not to be touched by their innocence. They are so helpless and in need of love that it is easy to reach out to help and to love.

Although they appear to be powerless, babies have a power all their own. They know how to hold their audience in thrall. They know how to reduce adults to cooing playing mates. They know how to turn off all the terrible anger of our daily struggles and bring us so much joy with only the silliest of smiles.

_____, you have entered our lives like a breath of fresh love. Your adoring audience of parents and grandparents surround you with admiration ready to record your slightest achievement with oohs and aahs! In your small body you represent the future, a picture of hopes and dreams waiting to be fulfilled.

May the Hebrew name you bear, _____, be a sign of your membership in the Jewish people and of your connection with all your ancestors. You have brought us so much happiness. We hope that you will do the same for yourself.

Rabbi Sherwin Wine

HOPE

When a child is born, hope is born. A baby makes us look forward with anticipation and excitement. So often we become prisoners of the past, dwelling on events we cannot change, filled with regret. But newborn children make us love the future, with all its possibilities and with all its opportunities. They unleash the power of our love and creativity and let us discover how much we need to nurture. When we give life to others, we give life to ourselves, we become alive with hope.

Your new son/daughter is the living expression of the power of your own love and the vitality of your own hope for the future.

May s/he give you dreams as s/he fulfills his/her own. May the name s/he bears, _____, always be a sign of the happy visions s/he inspires at this hour.

Rabbi Sherwin Wine

PARENTING

Love is ironic. It is never exhausted by use; it is stimulated by every new opportunity. Two people who love each other and who share in the creation and nurturing of a child find in this experience a special unity. Your child is the product of your love, and what s/he will become is the result of your consistency. Through your self-esteem, s/he will find his/her self-esteem. Though your compassion, s/he will find his/her compassion. Through your willingness to be free, s/he will desire to be free.

May your son/daughter, whom you have called _____, enrich and strengthen your love and may you ultimately give to him/her the respect that you feel for each other. May s/he take the gifts of your caring and make them a secure foundation for happiness and fulfillment.

Rabbi Sherwin Wine

TEACHING

We speak through our own behavior. Our lifestyle becomes a personal message. If we are generous, then our action teaches others how to be generous. If we are creative, then others can see how to be creative. If we are strong, then our strength becomes a vivid example to those around us. Good teachers teach by what they do, not by what they say. Good parents are good teachers. They mold the lives of their children by the beauty and integrity of their own actions.

May your new son/daughter learn from you what it means to be a loving and effective human being. Since you have the power to share yourselves with a newborn infant, you also have the power to give him/her the greatest and most intimate of all gifts-the gift of your loving behavior.

May the name s/he bears, _____, become the sign of the gentle virtue you so clearly value. It is your ultimate message to your child.

Rabbi Sherwin Wine

NAMING

In addition to welcoming _____(child's name)_____ into our community, we are today celebrating her/his place in our multicultural world by recognizing the multiple facets of her/his identity, including her/his Jewish name.

In ancient times, Jews gave their children Hebrew or Aramaic names. From the Middle Ages on, many Jewish children received Yiddish or Ladino names. As Jews settled in many places and we gave our children names in many languages, our custom has been to also give specifically Jewish names to our children.

Naming is often a ceremonial activity. Names are seen by many people as having magical powers, and thus naming is seen by them as a magical activity.

We humanists see in the poetry of naming expressions of connectedness - between earlier and later generations, between our images of the past and our hopes for the future.

As human beings have struggled to expand freedom and equality, we have also come to experience the way we name each other and ourselves as acknowledging or undermining the individuality and value of every person in the context of community and society.

Thus, the bestowing of names is part of what makes us more fully human.

Our ceremony today celebrates the abundance of meaning in the human search for personal and collective identities.

To help ____(child's English name)_____ explore the Jewish heritage that will form part of her/his identity, ____(parent name/s)___ have chosen to give her/him the Hebrew/Yiddish name/s: _____, and s/he/they is/are now going to share the stories behind that name and all the other names s/he is being given.

Rabbi Binyamin Biber

MEANING OF NAMES

A worthwhile moment during a naming or welcoming ceremony is to share with friends, family, and community the origin of the child's name. While the below examples are specific to past celebrations of the named individuals, they offer a template for use in future ceremonies.

Maia Ann Sheehan Kent

Jeff and Julie chose the name Maia to honor Jeff's Grandpa Max Werner. They hope Maia shares his qualities of peacefulness and inner strength. Maia shares her middle name, Ann, with her mother and Grammy Carol. She also carries Julie's family of origin name Sheehan. These names connect Maia to Julie's family.

In Hebrew, we have named Maia, Miriam (Miri-yam). Miriam comes from the Hebrew word that means bitterness from the sea. In knowing the bitterness in the world, may she be spared personal bitterness and be full of empathy for those who are inflicted with it. The biblical Miriam is the sister of the great prophet, Moses. It was Miriam's ingenuity that saved Moses from certain death as she placed him in the bulrushes to be discovered by the princess of Egypt. Miriam, a leader in her own right led the Israelites in dance, brandishing her tambourine, after they successfully crossed the Red Sea. Today, modern feminists have acknowledged her status as a prophetess and created Miriam's cup that now sits beside the cup of Elijah on the Seder table. May the heritage of the Biblical Miriam and the meaning of her name provide her with a balance of the characteristics of empathy, joy, compassion and leadership in her life and help her appreciate and know the fullness of all that life will bring her way.

Rabbi Miriam Jerris

Orli

Your name Orli comes from the Hebrew meaning 'my light'. Your parents chose this name because they not only liked its sound but loved its meaning. They want you to recognize and embrace the light that is in you and like your famous namesake, Orli Wald, the Angel of Auschwitz, your parents hope that you will live up to the meaning of your beautiful name by bringing light to everyone around you.

Rabbi Eva Goldfinger

James

Your parents chose to name you James to honour your mother's grandfather who was a gentle, humble and hardworking man who valued family above all else. By naming you after him your parents hope you will emulate his many fine qualities.

Rabbi Eva Goldfinger

Desmond/*Adam*

Desmond, your parents chose this name because they liked its sound, but its meaning also has significance. It comes from the French or Latin meaning the world or humankind—and that is the root of your Hebrew name Adam as well. Your parents want you to remember that you are part of all humankind and all are precious and worthy of your respect and support.

Rabbi Eva Goldfinger

Aaron Douglas Warrow

Scott and Susan have chosen the name Aaron in memory of Susan's maternal grandfather, Harry Borovitz, who was named Aharon, or Aaron in English. Susan had a special relationship with her grandpa. As a young child, she lived with her grandparents and she fondly remembers her Sunday morning breakfast sojourns with him. She recalls her grandpa and the twinkle in his eye. Harry was a small man, tough and athletic. He owned a bookstore. It is this wonderful combination of mind and body that Susan and Scott hope Aaron inherits from her Grandpa.

The Hebrew word Aharon means teaching or singing. It is also derived from the Hebrew to mean shining or mountain, or the Arabic to mean messenger. In the mythology of the Hebrew people, Aaron was the high priest, a leader of the Hebrew people. Since the name has multiple meanings in a variety of traditions, it is a good label for this multi-cultural little guy. Of course, Susan and Scott were drawn to the "teaching" meaning of his name since teaching is their chosen profession. May Aaron inherit the love of teaching and learning that his name reflects, and may he explore the many meanings he discovers and talents he develops in his life.

Scott and Susan chose Douglas for Aaron's middle name. Douglas is also Scott's middle name and that of his father. In choosing the middle name of Douglas, Scott and Susan are continuing this custom to the third generation. The word Douglas means "gray" in the Celtic tradition. Susan and Scott have chosen the Hebrew equivalent Kedar. It is their belief that one must know both black and white to achieve the balance of gray. Gray represents the coming together of the polarities. It represents the complexities that exist in life. In choosing the English and Hebrew names that reflect these ideas, we hope that Aaron Douglas will be prepared to know both ends of life experience, to know life fully. In acknowledging the gray or the shadow in himself, Aaron will be better prepared to accept the gray in others. It is in this understanding that Aaron Douglas will discover his capacity for empathy and compassion.

Rabbi Miriam Jerris

CHOOSING GUIDEPARENTS/ETHICAL MENTORS

In accordance with both Christian and Jewish traditions, (name of parents) have selected (name of guideparents) as Jacob's godparents. (To the guideparents), (name of parents) have chosen you as godparents because they believe you share similar life values and trust that you will play a significant and guiding role in (child's) life. For this reason, we will call you guideparents.

Rabbi Miriam Jerris

Ron and Shira

Ron and Shira, although the task of nurturing children belongs primarily to their parents, every person whose life touches this child will affect her. We all play a part in the development of this precious baby to her fullest potential. Shira's sister Aviva is intelligent, creative, passionate and charismatic. Ron's sister, Yoon has integrity and great imagination, she is dependable and is true to her passions as an artist. Both are caring and wonderful moms and they have therefore been chosen to represent us all as ethical mentors, the humanistic equivalent of godparents. Shira and Ron are delighted that they have accepted this responsibility.

Rabbi Eva Goldfinger

RECOGNITION OF OLDER SIBLING

Lilah wants her baby sister to know that she can always rely on her to have her back and that she will teach her everything she knows including how to have lots of fun. They will always be best sisters and friends. She also wants her to recognize how lucky she is to have Lilah as her big sister.

Rabbi Eva Goldfinger

Sam, this is a special time for you too. You are now a big brother. You can teach Jacob the things you know and help him learn about life. When a new baby comes home, your parents have to spend a lot of time feeding and taking care of the baby. Mommy and Daddy want to thank you for your patience and understanding, and your help. They want you to know how much they love you today and every day.

Rabbi Miriam Jerris

BAR OR BAT MITZVAH (B MITZVAH)

The terms Bar or Bat Mitzvah mean son or daughter of the commandment. Traditionally, it is a religious affirmation made by a young person who is now accepting responsibility for fulfilling the commandments of Yahweh, the Hebrew god. The Bat or Bar Mitzvah student typically reads a selection from the Torah and then a portion of the Haftorah connected to the particular Torah portion.

B Mitzvah is a gender neutral, inclusive term to denote both a Bat or a Bar Mitzvah. We encourage our members to use this respectful terminology. For Secular Humanistic Jews, the B Mitzvah is a coming of age ceremony for children who are thirteen years old or older. It allows the child to connect to their Jewish identity and study a person or topic that has significance to them and their families. Their study and ultimate presentation validate their values and enrich their lives, while connecting them to Jewish tradition. In Humanistic Judaism, parents and grandparents of any religion are full participants in the non-theistic ceremony created for and by the B Mitzvah student and her/his family.

GROWING UP

To be thirteen is to stand between two worlds, the past of childhood and the promise of adolescence. The middle years of teenage are often very hard to cope with. They are a testing ground for adult life. If we are too dependent on others, we must learn to become more independent. If we think too little of our talents, we must train ourselves to respect them. If we are afraid of the future, we must grow accustomed to live with the surprise of challenge.

Adolescence can be wasted in fear and laziness so that growing is too painful to bear. Or it can be a time of happy excitement when new responsibility becomes a pleasure and new learning becomes our hope for success.

Rabbi Sherwin Wine

MATURITY

Maturity is a balance of freedom and responsibility.

To the young, getting older seems attractive because of freedom. The older they become, the more they can choose their friends, what they wear, how they live their lives. Yet undisciplined freedom can lead to selfishness, greed, and isolation.

To adults, staying young seems attractive because of responsibility. The younger they were, the less responsible they were for their own lives and for the lives of others. Yet irresponsible adulthood robs us of dignity, and is no strategy for mature happiness.

Wisdom comes from the right balance of freedom and responsibility. We are free to choose our own path. The dignity of assuming responsibility provides a deep satisfaction, for the mastery of our own lives gives us the power to help others.

Rabbi Adam Chalom

INTEGRITY

Integrity is public and private, personal and social, words and deeds.

Integrity means that we say what we believe, and that we believe what we say. Our integrity affirms that we are the same person, in Hebrew and in English, synagogue and public square, special moments and any moment, holiday and every day. If our ancestors believed differently, we cherish their integrity as we do ours. When we agree, we find strength in honest roots. We honor them by celebrating our Judaism as deeply believed as they did.

We are what we say and what we do. Our intentions and emotions may be kind and generous. But if what we say and what we do are hurtful and hateful, no one will ever know our better nature. Indeed, our hands and our mouths speak the truth better than we realize. What we truly value, what we truly believe, we express in how we live.

Far easier to want to do good than to do it, to consider asking forgiveness than to ask. Far stronger to face our true selves, to acknowledge our failures, and to demand more. Integrity is not public perception. Integrity is integrating who we think we are with who we really are, transforming our ideal self into our actual self, making who we want to be the person we are becoming.

Rabbi Adam Chalom

ASSUMING RESPONSIBILITY

Some people spend their entire lives searching for the "meaning of life." Others come to understand that there is no singular "meaning of life." It is up to each of us to fashion meaning for our own lives.

We begin by setting goals and aspirations. But that is the easy part. Dreaming is important, but no one ever found purpose in life by simply dreaming. It takes hard work. If we are fortunate we will be helped along the way by family, friends and generous strangers.

Ultimately, we are responsible for reaching our own goals just as we are accountable for other aspects of our lives. It is challenging. It carries with it the risk of failures. But the rewards of assuming responsibility for determining our own unique purpose in life are worth it.

Rabbi Jeffrey Falick

THE CHAIN OF TRADITION FROM GENERATION TO GENERATION AND FAMILY TO FAMILY

The Jewish people have a very long history stretching back in time over 3500 years. The beginning of that history is rooted in the Middle East in the land of ancient Israel. During that period our ancestors were known first as Hebrews and then as Israelites.

Later, when our ancestors took on the name of Jews, they moved to many different countries, including the ancient lands of Babylonia, Greece, and Egypt. In more modern times, Jews moved on to still other countries, such as Russia and Germany, Spain, France, South Africa, Australia, China, the modern state of Israel and the United States.

According to our tradition, the history of the Jewish people began as the history of one family, the family of Abraham and Sarah. Over the years, going all the way to our own time, each generation has added a new chapter to that family history.

Many important values and beliefs have been passed down from generation to generation. At the same time, many other ideas and practices have been newly developed by each succeeding generation. So, there has been both continuity and change over the centuries.

Rabbi Peter Schweitzer

THE MEANING OF BAR/BAT MITZVAH

From birth to death, from cradle to grave, we mark the passages of life. These moments of transition and transformation are universal. They are part of the human experience.

We mark this journey in stages. From infancy to youth, from youth to young adulthood, from school to work to retirement, to parenthood perhaps, and grandparenthood, to old age, and then of course death, that final stage, which can come at any point along the way.

We enter the world with naming ceremonies and initiation rites. We depart with funeral rituals and memorials. Along the way, some mark birthdays, graduations, weddings, partnerships, anniversaries, and even divorces with other ceremonies and commemorations.

In traditional Jewish culture, children have been held fully accountable for their own deeds when they become thirteen, and assume religious and legal obligations according to ancient Jewish law. They are now called a bar or bat mitzvah, literally, the "son" or "daughter" of the commandments.

As Humanistic Jews, we recognize this transition to adulthood is a work in progress, as teenagers mature into young adults and their parents, in turn, entrust them with ever greater responsibilities of adulthood.

Rabbi Peter Schweitzer

ABOUT VALUES (VERSION 1)

The Bar/Bat Mitzvah service is a time to consider our values.

Humanistic Jews believe that any good value is a universal value. Jewish tradition has framed many good universal values in language that is unique to our culture. One of these is called *Tikkun Olam*, repairing the world.

Our world is imperfect. Everywhere we look we find conflict, hatred, abuse and intolerance. Many people feel that others should behave exactly according to the dictates of their own narrow world views. Others are selfishly invested in the accumulation of worldly goods even when it harms others.

If we focus on everything that is wrong with the world then we will raise up our hands in surrender. Trying to do too much overwhelms us and can only lead to despair. Instead, we must begin the process of *Tikkun Olam* with the one element of the world that is under control: our own behavior.

We must understand the effect that we each have on others and how that effect can ripple forward until it joins with others to form great waves of change. When we do so, we will be participating in the process of *Tikkun Olam*. It is a universal value in any language.

Rabbi Jeffrey Falick

ABOUT VALUES (VERSION 2)

The Bar/Bat Mitzvah service is a time to consider our values.

Humanistic Jews believe that any good value is a universal value. Jewish tradition has framed many good universal values in language that is unique to our culture. One of these is called *G'milut Chasadim*, performing deeds of loving kindness.

There are so many people in need. Some suffer from poverty. Hunger and want are their constant companions. They fear for their physical survival. Others suffer from discrimination. They are targeted because of the color of their skin, their family heritage, their beliefs or sexual orientation. Still others suffer from loneliness and abandonment, craving human companionship or even a kind word.

They all share one thing in common: an assault on their dignity. There exists only one cure: deeds of loving kindness.

We must work together to spread loving kindness throughout our societies. We must each take upon ourselves a commitment to demonstrate compassion, giving something of our substance and our capacity to care. When we do so, we will be practicing *G'milut Chasadim*- deeds of loving kindness. This is a universal value in any language.

Rabbi Jeffrey Falick

ABOUT VALUES (VERSION 3)

The Bar/Bat Mitzvah service is a time to consider our values.

Humanistic Jews believe that any good value is a universal value. Jewish tradition has framed many good universal values in language that is unique to our culture. One of these is called *Tzedakah*. Though *Tze-*

dakah is often translated as charity, it comes from the word for justice. Perhaps it is best understood as righteous assistance to others.

Every group of people organizes in order to help others. Whether we are working to feed the hungry, house the homeless, assist those with limitations, cure diseases or for any other positive objective, we accomplish more when we work collectively. For this purpose Jewish people, along with every other just society, have always formed charitable organizations to pool our financial resources and work for the common goal.

No individual person or group can change the world alone. But when we join hands in common cause we can see ourselves transforming it. Practicing *Tzedakah* is one of the best ways that we have discovered to pool our resources so that those who want to change the world will possess the means to do so. This is a universal value in any language.

Rabbi Jeffrey Falick

CHOOSING HEROES AND ROLE MODELS WHO EXEMPLIFY OUR VALUES

Becoming a bar or bat mitzvah is a time to choose values that we think are meaningful. It is also a time to identify who our heroes and roles models are because they stand for the values that are important to us.

Choosing heroes and role models means asking tough questions:

What makes a person worthy of our admiration?

Can someone still be a hero or role model if he or she has faults? After all, no one is perfect.

Does having a talent automatically make someone a role model or do one's talents need to be used in ways that make life better for others?

How can a role model influence our lives?

And finally, how can we become a role model for others and influence their lives?

Rabbi Peter Schweitzer

PUTTING VALUES INTO ACTION

It is one thing to talk about values and role models and to think about ways to make the world a better place. It is another thing to actually do something about it ourselves. Many people are all talk and little action. Some feel so overwhelmed at all the things that need to be done to improve our world that they don't know where to begin and so they don't do anything. That's where the words of Rabbi Tarfon are useful. He said:

It is not your duty to complete the task,
but nor are you free to desist from it. (Pirke Avot 2:21)

In other words, do what you can. One person, alone, isn't expected to make everything better, but if everyone works together, much can get done. Also, some tasks take a long time to finish, and what one person begins another may end up completing.

Rabbi Peter Schweitzer

READINGS BEFORE TORAH (VERSION 1)

Hand made
Man made;
Teller of stories
Maker of myths.

Unroll it.
Unbind it.
Approach it.
Unwind it.

Symbol of wisdom,
Source of tradition.
Look deep within it.
Find your own truth.

Rabbi Jodi Kornfeld

READINGS BEFORE TORAH (VERSION 2)

The beginning of wisdom is still wisdom.

The first brick in a foundation does not define a building, but without it, nothing would stand.

The first step down a path can still help us to see our ultimate goal.

Like the human heart, the Torah contains love and hate, violence and compassion, caring and cruelty. Like the Jewish experience, the Torah expresses the joy of community, the fear of the foreign, and the challenges of life. If it is the beginning of Jewish wisdom, it is neither the peak nor the end of our knowledge.

It is no wonder that this should be true. It was the Jewish experience, and human beings, that created the Torah. The Jewish people have read and interpreted, understood and misunderstood, imagined and re-created these passages in their own image from generation to generation.

Since the Torah's completion 2,500 years ago, humanity has progressed tremendously in ethics and philosophy, in law and literature.

Let us return to our first steps, that we might see where we may travel in our days.

Rabbi Adam Chalom

READINGS BEFORE TORAH (VERSION 3)

We give thanks for the privilege of reading from the Torah scroll, the most ancient literature of the Jewish People.

Morris Sukenik, Madrikh

MARRIAGE

Marriage is the legal affirmation and the emotional celebration of two equal partners who choose to spend their lives together. Humanistic Judaism, since its inception in the early 1960's, has warmly welcomed same-gender couples, multi-cultural couples, and couples from different religious backgrounds. Humanistic ceremonies are egalitarian and non-theistic. In a ceremony that equally honors both partners and both families, Secular Humanistic Jewish clergy will often participate in ceremonies co-officiated by a priest or minister from a different religious tradition or denomination. Each officiant has established their own guidelines for participating in non-traditional ceremonies.

ACCEPTING CHALLENGE

Marriage is an opportunity for happiness. It is also risky business. Two people who choose the partnership of love and loyalty need many skills to make it work. They need patience, kindness, generosity, good humor, and the ability to compromise. They need persistence, nurturing trust, discretion, and the willingness to be vulnerable.

But almost nothing offers a greater possibility for living life well. When marriage works it justifies all the effort. Life is richer when experience is shared. We are more ourselves when we are responding to the stimulus of others, especially when we are responding to the gift of love. Good lovers bring out the best in each other.

If romance leads to friendship, if coming together makes room for individual space, if dreams turn into realistic expectations, if the dazzle of beginnings yields to long-run commitment, if one is always willing to demand of oneself what one demands of others, then love becomes more profound and the bond of marriage is strengthened.

To choose marriage is to accept a challenge, the challenge that love provides when it wants to grow.

Rabbi Sherwin Wine

PARTNERSHIP

Marriage is a partnership. It is not a merger in which two people lose their individual identities. It is not a union of master and servant. It is a commitment, reinforced by love, of equals who discover that they are more fulfilled together than they are apart. In a good marriage husband and wife are aware of how much they need each other—of how much they transform each other. Joy, laughter, caring, tenderness, and hope are the gifts of love. In the presence of loneliness and strangers it is difficult to express all that we are. In the presence of love we feel our power and experience life in a new way. And you are partners in love who taste life more fully because you have found each other.

Rabbi Sherwin Wine

SELF-DISCOVERY

Loneliness is not the best of human conditions. Although being alone is sometimes necessary and desirable, being alone all the time undermines the human spirit and prevents us from being what we ought to be. We are people needing people. We are social beings in search of human contact. We are persons reaching out, seeking completeness in the encounter with those we love. In the presence of friends and lovers we discover more about ourselves. We come to understand our need to touch, our need to communicate, our need to share.

Marriage is the celebration of our basic human needs. If it is good, it does not limit us. It does not restrict our freedom; rather it fulfills it. It takes our power to love and to share and channels it into long-run satisfaction. Bonds of loyalty and commitment allay our fear of being vulnerable and open up to us the pleasures of intimacy. In marriage we become friends and partners in the exploration of ourselves and the world we live in.

Rabbi Sherwin Wine

MEANING OF MARRIAGE

Marriage is a sacred act. It consists of entrusting our deepest selves into the loving care of another. It is a public and legal act to be sure. It is also an emotional and spiritual act. The spiritual aspect of marriage must be embraced openly, seriously, and completely for the marriage to endure. Partner 1 and partner 2 commit themselves today to each other in sacred trust. They promise to embrace conflict as well as peace; to work as well as play; to struggle as well as thrive; to give as well as receive; and to be with, stay with, and move toward one another.

Rabbi Miriam Jerris

Partner 1 and Partner 2 view marriage as a coming together at all levels of being – mind, body, and spirit. A marital commitment includes the willingness to be open and vulnerable, and the courage to take risks. Marriage is a conscious act of will. To remain in marriage we must continually renew our will to be married. Marital partners accept the challenges that living together in love offers. They decide that they will face the fears that are a necessary part of establishing and growing an intimate relationship. And you, partner 2 and partner 1 have made the commitment to create and recreate this conscious partnership. Those of us who are married or in relationships may take this moment to consciously reaffirm our commitment to our partners, and those of us who are currently unattached may take this moment to reaffirm our commitment to ourselves and our loved ones.

Rabbi Miriam Jerris

INTERCULTURAL MARRIAGE

Often people feel that religious differences between two people who are about to marry may be an obstacle to their happiness. I have a slightly different point of view that I often share with the couples that I work with during their marriage ceremony.

All marriages are mixed marriages. All marriage partners are different in some ways. They may differ in the way they spend money or the way they resolve conflicts or in their sleeping patterns. But I guarantee that there is not one couple on this earth that would say that they agree on everything.

Couples who come together from different religious, cultural, or ethnic backgrounds acknowledge their differences immediately. They learn skills of negotiation to cope with their differences. And these are the exact skills that are needed in all marriages. Intercultural couples can be stronger than other couples who share their backgrounds. Often couples who share their ethnic, religious, and cultural backgrounds can be lulled into a kind of complacency because their differences may not be so obvious.

The cultural life of an intermarried couple can also be more enriched than those who share backgrounds. Diversity keeps life interesting. We can always enjoy the things we share. It takes special people who can learn to celebrate their differences — special people like you.

Rabbi Miriam Jerris

AUTUMN

As the heat of summer gives way to the cool of fall, we enter the most glorious season of the year. This is the time of year with the most surprise. We feel the expectation of change. We can be treated to splendid sunny days, reminiscent of summer. We can delight in the delicious freshness of autumn. We glimpse winter in the cold rains. We anticipate the leaves turning color to reveal their full grandeur. In this time of change, we appreciate the excitement of possibilities and the majesty yet unseen. May your marriage reflect the complexity and fullness of this season. May you always recall its splendor and potential even as you glimpse the cold winter rains. May your joy be reflected in the brilliance of change and promise.

Rabbi Miriam Jerris

EXCHANGE OF RINGS AND VOW TO CHILD

It is traditional to exchange tokens of some value in order to make your promises legal and binding. The double-ring ceremony that you have chosen signifies that your marriage is a partnership, with mutuality of respect and equality of status.

Like a circle without beginning or end, these rings, which you are about to exchange, symbolize continuity, security and harmony, all of which we wish upon your marriage.

David, place this ring on Jennifer's finger and say, "Jennifer, with this ring we are united in love and loyalty." Now share your personal words of love and devotion that will join you as husband and wife.

Jennifer, place this ring on David's finger and say, "David, with this ring we are united in love and loyalty." Now share your personal message of caring and commitment that will unite you as wife and husband.

Now holding hands and looking into each other's eyes, would you share the ancient words of love from Song of Songs with one another.

Jennifer, repeat after me, "I am for my beloved and my beloved is for me". David, would you respond, "I am for my beloved and my beloved is for me."

Katherine would you join us up here please.

David and Jennifer, today you have exchanged vows of love and loyalty with one another, but Katherine is an elemental part of your lives and you would like to make a personal vow to her as well. Would the two of you please take the special 'creating a family' pendant and put it around Katherine's neck then share your family vows with her.

May the love which you have declared for each other, reach out to include your cherished family and friends, who are a circle of strength and love that can grow continually. Each crisis faced together makes the circle stronger, and every joy shared, strengthens the bonds of love.

Rabbi Eva Goldfinger

RINGS

The rings you are about to give and receive are symbols of the vows you have just made to one another. They symbolize the eternity of time and love that has no beginning and no ending. Remember, however, that no tangible symbol can ever substitute for loving behavior. Your treatment of each other will always be the sign of your commitment.

Partner 1, place this ring on Partner 2 finger and repeat after me: Hare at/ m'ku'deshet li/ b'tabaat zo/ k'minhagei umot ha-olam./ Be thou consecrated unto me/ with this ring/ as my wife/according to the customs of the world's people./ Ani l'dodatee, v'dodatee, lee. I am my beloved's and my beloved is mine.

Partner 2, place this ring on Partner 1 finger and repeat after me: Hare ata/ m'kudash li/ b'tabaat zo/ k'minhagei umot ha-olam. Be thou consecrated unto me/ with this ring/ as my husband/ according to the according to the customs of the world's people./ "Ani l'dodi v'dodi li. I am my beloved's and my beloved is mine.

Rabbi Miriam Jerris, Hebrew adapted by Rabbi Jeffrey Falick

CHILDREN IN WEDDING CEREMONIES — CANDLELIGHTING

Alexander, Rachel and Alex, would you please join us for the candle lighting ceremony.

Fire is one of nature's basic elements. To our ancient ancestors it was the source of life itself. It is therefore no surprise that throughout the ages fire and light have retained their eminence in celebrations of all peoples. In all traditions fire symbolizes love, enlightenment, and the ethical values we pass down from generation to generation. At the beginning of this ceremony, I lit a heritage candle representing all of these.

Jeilah and Gary, would you each take an unlit candle from the table. To symbolically accept the torch of the values and heritage passed down to you, would you each light your candles by putting them into the flame of the heritage candle.

Gary, Jeilah, these flames which you now hold represent the essence and entirety of each of you; your heritage—where you come from, your values—what you believe and are now, and your spirit—which is all that you can be. When two people join their lives, they bring together all that they were and are. Once together however, the potential for each to grow and blossom, is dramatically enhanced.

Would you now put your flames together and light the woven candle that represents your unity. The light of your love and spirits is now joined in a single flame.

Alexander, Rachel and Alex would you each pick up an unlit candle from the table.

Jeilah and Gary, would you please pick up the unity candle, hold it together, and to symbolically pass the torch of your values, heritage and love down to Alexander, Rachel and Alex would you light their candles now.

May the brightness of your candles shine throughout your lives, giving you courage and reassurance in the darkness. May that light, through your dedication, help illuminate the darker corners of our world and contribute to the repair of our world.

Rabbi Eva Goldfinger

CUP OF UNITY/WINE CEREMONY

This goblet is a single cup from which you shall drink. It is a sign of your unity. Although you are two distinct persons, both respecting the equal dignity of the other, you have chosen to unite your lives and to seek your happiness together. You drink from the same cup to be reminded that you will share pain and pleasure, struggle and success.

ASHRAY HEHATAN V'HAKALLA SHEYIMTS'OO AHAVA B'NISSOOEEN.
Happy are a man and a woman who find love in marriage.

Take this cup and drink from it in the spirit of loving union.

Rabbi Sherwin Wine

SHEVA BRAKHOT/SEVEN BLESSINGS (VERSION 1)

1) We are blessed by the glory and beauty of all the universe.
ANOO M'VORAKHIM AL YADAY HOD HA-OLAM.

Congregation – "LOO Y'HEE" or "May it Be"

2) We are blessed by the wonder and miracle of human existence.
ANOO M'VORAKHIM AL YADAY P'LIAT HA-KHAYIM.

Congregation – "LOO Y'HEE" or "May it Be"

3) We are blessed to be individuals drawn to each other for love, companionship, family, and future.
ANOO M'VORAKHIM AL YADAY AHAVATEYNU, EKHAD EL HA-SHEYNI.

Congregation – "LOO Y'HEE" or "May it Be"

4) We are blessed to celebrate the joy of the Jewish people and of all peoples for new love and for new life. We rejoice for our children.
ANOO M'VORAKHIM AL YADAY SIMKHAT B'NAY ADAM L'AHAVA U'L'KHAYIM.

Congregation – "LOO Y'HEE" or "May it Be"

5) We are blessed to enact the human drama of finding love and marriage in our lifetimes, as humanity has from the beginning. When we love, it is as pure as Eden, as joyful as Paradise.

ANOO M'VORAKHIM LIMTZO AHAVAH V'KHUPPAH K'V'RESHIT.

Congregation – "LOO Y'HEE" or "May it Be"

6) We are blessed by joy and gladness, groom and bride, mirth, singing, pleasure, delight, love, brotherhood, peace and companionship. May there be heard in the cities of Judah and the streets of Jerusalem the sound of joy and the sound of gladness – קוֹל שָׂשׂוֹן קוֹל שִׂמְחה, the voice of the groom and the voice of the bride - קוֹל חתן וקוֹל כלה. We are blessed by the love of bride and groom.

ANOO M'VORAKHIM AL YADAY SASSON V'SIMKHA, KHATAN V'KALAH, AHAVA V'AKHAVA, SHALOM V'RE'UT. ANOO M'VORAKHIM AL YADAY AHAVAT KHATAN EEM HA-KALAH.

Congregation – "LOO Y'HEE" or "May it Be"

Rabbi Adam Chalom

7) Wine Blessing
SAVRI MARAN V'RABANAN D'ETMOL: KIDASHNU ET HA-YAYIN

SAVRI MARAN V'RABANAN D'HAYOM: BRUKHIM BOREY P'RI HA-GAFEN.

The Rabbis and Sages of old proclaimed: we sanctify this wine.

The Rabbis and Sages of today proclaim: blessed is the fruit of the vine.

Congregation - L'KHAYIM! To Life!

Morris Sukenik, Madrikh

SHEVA BRAKHOT/SEVEN BLESSINGS (VERSION 2)

It is traditional at Jewish weddings to express our joy, hopes and blessings for the bride and groom by reciting seven blessings or sheva brakhot:

1. We are grateful for the eternal unfolding of the seasons which has brought us to this momentous occasion.

ANU MODIM SHEHECHEYANU, V'KIY'MANU V'HIGI-YANU LAZMAN HAZE.

2. We rejoice in our heritage and in the blessing of life's passages that bring both joy and sorrow and offer challenge and opportunity.

ASHRAYNU BIY'RUSHATAYNU U'BIVRAKHOT N'KU-DOT HATZIYUN B'CHAYIM.

3. Radiant is the spirit in humankind that illuminates our world through establishing justice and peace.

BARUKH HAOR B'ADAM SHEHAYVI TZEDEK V'SHA-LOM LAOLAM.

4. Empowering is the potential in human beings to combine love, wisdom, and courage and to forge a better life for themselves and their loved ones.

B'RUKHA HAY'KHOLET B'ADAM.

5. Precious is the love and support of family, friends and community

B'RUKHA T'MIKHAT HAMISHPACHA, HACHAVERIM, V'HAK'HILA.

6. Blessed is the happiness of groom and bride who share in joy and gladness, pleasure and exultation, love and harmony, peace and friendship.

B'RUKHA SIMCHAT CHATAN V'KALA, GILA, RINA, DITZA, V'CHEDVA, AHAVA, V'ACHAVA, V'SHALOM, V'RAYUT.

7. We rejoice with _____ and _____. May they find ever-increasing joy as they devote themselves to growing and sharing, and nurturing and supporting one another.

ANU SMAYCHIM IM _____ V'_____. N'VARAYKH ET HACHATAN V'ET HAKALA.

Rabbi Eva Goldfinger

MEMORIALS / FUNERALS

Secular Humanistic funerals and memorials are designed to celebrate the life of the individual who has died and to provide comfort based on reality to those mourning. We know that people live on in us through the memories we have and share. Our approach is one that affirms what we know about life and death through scientific evidence. The Kaddish, a prayer extolling the greatness of a divine being that is traditionally used during funerals and memorials, including memorial moments during Shabbat and holidays, has been rewritten by a number of Secular Humanistic rabbis and leaders to affirm life in the face of death.

WELCOME/INTRODUCTION TO A MEMORIAL SERVICE

Dear family and friends. We have come together to pay tribute and honor the life of (Name), mother, sister, aunt and dear friend. We gather fully aware of the value of love and support that comes from the gathering of family and friends. And although (name) died three weeks ago, the loss and sadness are still startlingly palpable. We know that in speaking the sadness publicly and sharing what we feel, we take one more step on the path that leads to healing. In sharing our memories, we find our strength in ourselves and through each other. Contrary to popular opinion, time does not heal all wounds. Time is neutral. It is what we do with time that matters. Healing comes as we grieve and as we support each other in our mourning. That is why we are together.

Rabbi Miriam Jerris

MEMORY

No one event can encapsulate a life. No one service can heal the pain of loss. The most to be hoped is that each stage of the journey is a step toward living life anew, a step in favor of love and vitality and the beauty of the world and the people around us.

We who survive are the keepers of memory. Grief may return at unexpected moments— a family event, a special transition, or even an ordinary day can become an instant of sadness. And that is entirely as it should be. For we do not forget our loved ones; at best we become accustomed to the world without their presence.

The light of life burns on.

Rabbi Adam Chalom

COURAGE

Death needs courage. It is so overwhelmingly final that it fills our lives with dread and anxious fear. When it arrives at the end of a long and happy life it is never welcome, yet not deeply resented. But when it comes too soon, invading young lives, disrupting hopes and dreams, it adds anger to our fear. We cry out at the injustice of destiny and wait for answers that never seem to come.

Courage is the power to confront a world that is not always fair. It is the refusal to beg for what will never be given. It is the willingness to accept what cannot be changed. Courage is loving life even in the face of death. It is sharing our strength with others even when we feel weak. It is embracing our family and friends even when we fear to lose them. It is opening ourselves to love, even for the last time. Courage is self-esteem. It prefers quiet determination to whining. It prefers doing to waiting. It affirms that exits, like entrances, have their own dignity.

_____, whom we loved very much and still do, chose to die with dignity. We shall never forget his/her courage.

Rabbi Sherwin Wine

FAMILY

Life offers the gift of many blessings. None is more precious than the love of family and friends. In the strength and compassion of parents, in the mutual devotion of husband and wife, brother and sister, we find the security of love. For the landscape of our years is peopled by the presence of open hearts that exact no price for the gift of themselves. When an intimate friend dies, sadness and despair are normal responses. Two people cannot share the best and worst of life in mutual experience and find that absence is trivial. The tribute of love is the pain of separation.

Rabbi Sherwin Wine

TRAGEDY

The past is unchangeable. What happened yesterday is beyond our control. We can cry and shout, we can scream and complain, but the events of just a moment ago are as far from our reach as the farthest star. Fools never forgive the past. They devote every present moment to worrying about it, scolding it and wishing it were different. Wise people release the past. They do not need to assault what cannot be taken. They do not need to forgive what cannot be altered. They simply accept what they are not able to change. Since the future is open to human decision, they turn their energies forward and choose to create rather than to regret. People of self-respect do not dwell on helplessness. They do not assault what cannot be taken. Since death is irreversible, they accept it and turn to living.

Rabbi Sherwin Wine

DEFIANCE

Death is a reminder of human frailty. We are very vulnerable creatures. And we have so many natural enemies. Floods and earthquakes, disease and famine, heat and cold take their toll and thin our ranks. Even in the time of science the ancient enemies of aging and decay still creep up on us uninvited and make us mortal.

Even when the world is at peace there is still a war to be fought – not a war of people against people – but a war against death and all its friends. If we must fight, let us fight poverty. If we must enter battle, let us battle with disease. If we must assault the enemy, let us assault the poisons of our environment. There are many real foes to face.

Let our tribute to the dead be our struggle against death.

Rabbi Sherwin Wine

DIGNITY

The value of life does not lie in mere survival. Lasting eternally is never enough. The value of life lies in personal dignity. Self-respect, however brief, gives human existence its meaning.

The long life of cautious boredom is inferior to the short life of bold adventure. Many of us who believe ourselves to be living are already dead. And many who have died live on in the memory of their courage.

Rabbi Sherwin Wine

HOPE

I believe.
I believe in hope.
I believe in hope that chooses – that chooses self-respect above pity.
I believe in hope that dismisses – that dismisses the petty fears of petty people.
I believe in hope that feels – that feels distant pleasure as much as momentary pain.
I believe in hope that acts – that acts without the guarantee of success.
I believe in hope that kisses – that kisses the future with the transforming power of its will.

Hope is a choice,
never found,
never given,
always taken.

Some wait for hope to capture them.
They act as the prisoners of despair.
Others go searching for hope.
They find nothing but the reflection of their own anger.

Hope is an act of will,
affirming, in the presence of evil,
that good things will happen,
preferring in the face of failure, self-esteem to pity.

Optimists laugh, even in the dark
They know that
hope is a life-style –
not a guarantee.

Rabbi Sherwin Wine

HAIKU

I hear in my heart
the music of memory
the song of my soul.

Ruth Duskin Feldman, Madrikha

YOUR VOICE

I lost your voice.
I lost your timbre, your cadence, your accent.

I lost your voice.
I had it the first month.
I had it the first year.
Then it faded.
Then it was gone.

I lost your voice.
I can't hear it anymore.

I lost your voice,
But not your words.
Your words of approval.
Your words of wisdom.
Your words of support, of love, of guidance.

I lost your voice,
But I'll always have your words.

Arthur Liebhaber

IN MEMORIAM

I got a promotion,
I started to make the call,
Then I remembered.

I got sick and didn't know what to do,
I started to make the call,
Then I remembered.

I forgot what that Yiddish expression meant,
I started to call,
Then I remembered.

I wanted your recipe,
I started to call,
Then I remembered.

Good news, bad news,
Wisdom and guidance,
I start to make the calls,
But then I remember.

You aren't out there,
You aren't going to answer.
You're in my heart,
I'll always remember.

Arthur Liebhaber

REMEMBERING OUR LOVED ONES

We take this time to remember our loved ones who shared their wisdom with us by word and by example.

We remember them as their words echo in our ears. We remember them as we picture them in our mind's eye. We remember them each time we notice them in ourselves, saying what they would say, gesturing in the way they would gesture.

We remember their tears and their laughter. We remember their hope and despair. We remember their anger and their praise. We remember their achievements and their failures. We remember their jokes and stories. We remember their disappointments and triumphs.

We remember the things they did and the things left undone. Most of all we remember their gentle words and soft touch and all the silent unspoken ways they affected us, and we give thanks for their presence in our lives.

Rabbi Miriam Jerris

MODERN KADDISH / GLORY OF LIFE

May the glory of life be extolled. L'chaim.

May the world be blessed with peace, all life hallowed by love and respect. L'chaim.

Let life be blessed, and glorified, exalted and honored. L'chaim.

Though beyond praises, songs, and adorations we may utter, let life be celebrated. L'chaim.

For us, for all Israel, for all people, may the promise and the gift of life come true. L'chaim.

May peace embrace all of us, all Israel, and all the world. L'chaim.

May peace be granted us, we who mourn, and be a comfort to all who are bereaved, and let us say, L'chaim.

Zay-cher tza-dee-keem lee-v'ra-kha. May the memory of good people be for us a blessing (*Proverbs 10:7*)

Rabbi Peter Schweitzer

HUMANISTIC MOURNER'S QADDISH
QADDISH YATOM

"Qaddish Yatom" literally means "Dedication / Devotion of an Orphan."
This Humanistic memorial reading is based on the traditional Qaddish which is recited by mourners in a group setting - traditionally in a "minyan" of ten Jewish men. This particular all-English version is designed for reading alone or with loved ones at home.

As we now remember our loved ones who have died, all of us able stand in their honor and offer this affirmation of our "dedication," our qaddish, to life and its improvement.

Let us remember our loved ones in all their humanity, with all their strengths and limitations.

As we learn from their lives, let us bless and praise their memories with our actions.

Let us remember them in their glory and at their heights.

May we carry on the best elements of their lives with splendor.

May we ascend in the shining examples of their praiseworthy deeds.

Let us dedicate ourselves in honoring the best legacies of our loved ones' past for the sake of all those who now live and for the sake of all those who will yet come to live in this world.

May it be our heart's desire to work for healing and equity, for freedom and peace - to cultivate these in our lives, and in our days, and in the lives of everyone in the world, swiftly and soon.

And let us say: "Amen."

Even as we speak, we know that the value of each life exceeds what can be expressed in blessings or in songs, in praises or in words of consolation.

In remembering the loved ones for whom we mourn, may we find lessons and inspiration in their legacies.

Let us remember righteous actions for blessing.

And let us say: "Amen."

Rabbi Binyamin Biber

HUMANISTIC KADDISH

Let us enhance and exalt ourselves in the spirit of humanity.

Let us acclaim the preciousness of life.

Let us show gratitude for life by approaching it with reverence.

Let us embrace the whole world, even as we wrestle with its parts.

Let us, each in our own way, take up our share in serving the world and seeking truth.

May our commitment to life help us to strengthen healing of spirit and peace of mind.

May healing and peace permeate and comfort all of Israel and all those who dwell on earth.

And let us say:

Ken y'hi...May it be so.

Jon Dickman and Congregation Kol Shalom, inspired by Rabbi Rami Shapiro

CLOSING

Memory is a precious possession. It captures the past and trains it to our need. The harshness of old events is softened by vagueness and the pleasures of happy moments are sharpened by vivid imagination. Loved ones linger on in the glory of their individual uniqueness. In life they willed to live and hewed the path of their personal difference. In death they transcend decay and find their niche in fond remembrance. No person is defined by the sameness of another. If it were so, memory would die from generalities.

In the particular grace of _____ lies his/her immortality. May the memory of _____, whom we loved in life and still love in death, bless our thoughts and actions. May the special grace of his/her years reach out to touch our hearts and to give us hope.

Rabbi Sherwin Wine

BIBLIOGRAPHY: LIFE CYCLES

Barker, Dan. *Maybe Right, Maybe Wrong: A Guide for Young Thinkers*. Buffalo, NY: Prometheus Books, 1992.

Barker, Dan. *Maybe Yes, Maybe No: A Guide for Young Skeptics*. Buffalo, N.Y.: Prometheus Books, 1993.

Bennett, Helen. *Humanism, What's That? A Book for Curious Kids*. Amherst, N.Y.: Prometheus Books, 2005.

Byock, Ira. *Dying Well: Peace and Possibilities at the End of Life*. New York: Riverhead Books, 1997.

Jackson, Buzzy. *The Inspirational Atheist: Wise Words on the Wonder and Meaning of Life*. New York: Plume, 2014.

Lerner, Devon. *Celebrating Interfaith Marriages*. New York: Henry Holt, 1999.

McGowan, Dale, Molleen Matsumura, Amanda Metskas, and Jan Dover. *Raising Freethinkers: A Practical Guide for Parenting Beyond Belief*. New York: AMACOM, 2009.

Moss, Lisa Braver and Rebecca Wald. *Celebrating Brit Shalom*. Oakland, CA: Notim Press, 2015.

Petsonk, Judy and Jim Remsen. *The Intermarriage Handbook*. New York: Arbor House, William Morrow, 1988.

Remen, Rachel Naomi. *My Grandfather's Blessings: Stories of Strength, Refuge, and Belonging*. New York: Riverhead Books, 2000.

Roberts, Elizabeth and Robert Amidon. *Life Prayers: 365 Prayers, Blessings and Affirmations to Celebrate the Human Journey*. New York: Harper Collins, 1996.

Riemer, Jack and Nathaniel Stampfer. *So That Your Values Live On: Ethical Wills and How to Prepare Them*. Woodstock, Vermont: Jewish Lights Publishing, 1991.

Schwartz, Barry L. *Jewish Heroes Jewish Values: Living Mitzvot in Today's World*. U.S.: Behrman House, Inc., 1996.

Searl, Edward. *In Memoriam: A Guide to Modern Funeral and Memorial Services*. Boston, MA: Skinner House Books, 2000.

Society for Humanistic Judaism, "Celebrating Life's Passages," *Humanistic Judaism*, (Winter/Spring 1999).

Society for Humanistic Judaism, "Coming of Age: The Bar and Bat Mitzvah," *Humanistic Judaism*, (1982).

Society for Humanistic Judaism, "Intermarriage," *Humanistic Judaism*, (Spring/Summer 2003)

Society for Humanistic Judaism, "A Parenting Primer for Humanistic Jews," *Humanistic Judaism*, (Autumn 2012/Winter-Spring 2013)

Strom, Margot Stern. *Facing History and Ourselves: Holocaust and Human Behavior.* Brookline, MA: Facing History and Ourselves National Foundation, Inc., 1994.

Suneby, Liz and Diane Heiman. *The Mitzvah Project Book: Making Mitzvah Part of Your Bar/Bat Mitzvah… and Your Life.* Woodstock, Vermont: Jewish Lights Publishing, 2011.

Westridge Young Writers Workshop. *Kids Explore America's Jewish Heritage.* Santa Fe, NM: John Muir Publications, 1996.

Wine, Sherwin T. *Celebration: A Ceremonial and Philosophic Guide for Humanists and Humanistic Jews.* Buffalo, New York: Prometheus Books, 1988.

Wolfelt, Alan D. *Understanding Your Grief.* Fort Collins, CO: Companion, 2003.

CONTRIBUTORS

Dr. Jerald Bain, Madrikh, a founding member of Oraynu Congregation, Toronto, Ontario.

Rabbi Binyamin Biber, Humanist Chaplain at American University and former rabbi of Machar, The Washington Congregation for Secular Humanistic Judaism, in Washington DC.

Rabbi Adam Chalom, Ph.D., rabbi of Kol Hadash Humanistic Congregation, Lincolnshire, Illinois, and Dean for North America of the International Institute for Secular Humanistic Judaism.

Jon Dickman, past chair of Ritual Committee, Kol Shalom Community for Humanistic Judaism in Portland, Oregon.

Ruth Duskin Feldman, *z'l*, Madrikha and former editor of *Humanistic Judaism,* was a member of Kol Hadash Humanistic Congregation in Lincolnshire, Illinois.

Rabbi Jeffrey Falick, rabbi of The Birmingham Temple, Congregation for Humanistic Judaism, in Farmington Hills, Michigan.

Natan Fuchs, member and teacher at The Birmingham Temple, Congregation for Humanistic Judaism, in Farmington Hills, Michigan.

Rabbi Eva Goldfinger, Life Cycle Director and Adult Educator, Oraynu Congregation for Humanistic Judaism, in Toronto, Ontario.

Rabbi Denise Handlarski, Ph.D., rabbi of Oraynu Congregation for Humanistic Judaism, in Toronto, Ontario.

Rabbi Miriam Jerris, Ph.D., rabbi of the Society for Humanistic Judaism and Associate Professor of Professional Development of the International Institute for Secular Humanistic Judaism.

Rabbi Jodi Kornfeld, rabbi of Beth Chaverim Humanistic Jewish Community, in Deerfield, Illinois.

Rabbi Jeremy Kridel, rabbi of Machar, The Washington Congregation for Secular Humanistic Judaism, in Washington, D.C., and editor of *Humanistic Judaism* Magazine.

Laurence Levine, *z'l*, was a member of The Birmingham Temple, Congregation for Humanistic Judaism, in Farmington Hills, Michigan.

Arthur Liebhaber, member of The Birmingham Temple, Congregation for Humanistic Judaism, in Farmington Hills, Michigan, and the Secretary/Treasurer of the Society for Humanistic Judaism.

Rabbi Sivan Malkin Maas, Dean of Tmura, the Rabbinic Seminary for Secular Humanistic Judaism in Israel.

Marilyn Rowens, Madrikha, member of The Birmingham Temple,

Congregation for Humanistic Judaism, in Farmington Hills, Michigan.

Rabbi Peter Schweitzer, rabbi emeritus of The City Congregation for Humanistic Judaism, in New York, New York.

Rabbi Judith Seid, rabbi of Tri-Valley Cultural Jews, in Greater East Bay, California.

Rabbi Ayala Shanee, operation manager of IISHJ Tmura – Israeli Judaism.

Morris Sukenik, *z'l*, Madrikh, was the first leader of the Queens Society for Humanistic Judaism in Queens, NY.

Rabbi Frank Tamburello, rabbi of the Westchester Community for Humanistic Judaism, in Westchester, New York.

Rabbi Sherwin Wine, *z'l*, was the founder of Secular Humanistic Judaism and its national organizations, including the Society for Humanistic Judaism and the International Institute for Secular Humanistic Judaism, and was the founder and rabbi emeritus of The Birmingham Temple, Congregation for Humanistic Judaism, in Farmington Hills, Michigan.

ORGANIZATIONS AND WEBSITES

Association of Humanistic Rabbis. (www.humanisticrabbis.org). Rabbinical organization for the Secular Humanistic Jewish Movement.

British Humanist Association (https://humanism.org.uk/store/ceremonies-books/). Books on Baby Welcoming Ceremonies, Weddings and Funerals and Memorials available for purchase.

Congress of Secular Jewish Organizations (www.csjo.org). Secular Jewish organization partners with SHJ in the IISHJ.

International Institute for Secular Humanistic Judaism (https://iishj.org). Educational arm for the Secular Humanistic Jewish Movement.

Ritual Well (https://www.ritualwell.org). Ritual website for the Reconstructionist Movement for Holidays and Life Cycles. Material may need to be adapted for use in Humanistic Judaism.

Society for Humanistic Judaism (https://shj.org). Community-organizing and advocacy/outreach arm for the Humanistic Judaism movement.

Special thanks to the board and staff of the
SOCIETY FOR HUMANISTIC JUDAISM
for their leadership and assistance on this project

BOARD

EXECUTIVE COMMITTEE
Richard D. Logan, President
Mary Raskin, Vice President
Arthur Liebhaber, Secretary & Treasurer
Larry M. Lawrence, Past President

Marlene Cohen, Andrea Friedlander, Susan Herschman, Victoria Ratnaswamy, Susan Ryan, Sheila Sebor

DIRECTORS
Roger Addelson, Zachary Barnett, Darlene Basch, Stephanie Blum, Bill Brostoff, Paula Creed, Stuart Dolnick Jeff Friedman, Lisa Gardner-Springer, Rick Gold, Evelyn Goldstein, Allen Gorrelick, Sue Greenspan, Lee Jacobi, Erica Jonlin, Rob Lasker, Jon Levine, Sheila Malcolm, Janet Mayer, E. Ronald Milan, George Molnar, Dana Preis, Susan Rubin, Amy Schneider, Barry Swan, Frank Tamburello, Susan Warrow

HUJEWS YOUTH COUNCIL
Areya Campbell-Rosen, Aliza Kopans, Sam Greenberg, Libby Otto

STAFF

EXECUTIVE DIRECTOR
Paul Golin

RABBI
Miriam Jerris

INFORMATION MANAGER
Jennifer Grodsky

ADMINISTRATIVE ASSISTANT
Kathy Tschirhart

EDITOR, HUMANISTIC JUDAISM
Rabbi Jeremy M. Kridel

HUJEWS CONCLAVE COORDINATOR
Anna Goldberg

PAST PRESIDENTS

1970-1973 Robert Poris
Ocala FL

1973-1975 John Franklin *

1975-1977 Dr. Gerald Berman

1977-1978 Margery Buxbaum
Crossville, TN

1978-1981 (Rabbi) Miriam Jerris
Huntington Woods, MI

1981-1983 James Reiter
Milford, MI

1983-1985 Jeffrey Schesnol
Phoenix, AZ

1985-1987 Leonard Cherlin *

1987-1990 Lynne Master
Huntington Woods, MI

1990-1992 Robert Sandler
Commerce Township, MI

1992-1994 Rosalyn Hill
Fairfield, CT

1994-1996 Dana Wolfe Naimark
Phoenix, AZ

1996-1998 **Rick Naimark**
Phoenix, AZ

1998-2000 **Bert Steinberg** *

2000-2001 **Toby Dorfman**
San Marcos, CA

2001-2003 **Shari Gelber**
Newton Centre, MA

2003-2006 **Phil Gould** *

2006-2012 **Louis Altman**
Minneapolis, MN

2012-2014 **Andrea Friedlander**
Deerfield, IL

2014-2016 **Larry M. Lawrence**
Washington, DC

2016- **Richard D. Logan**
Minneapolis, MN

* Deceased

SHERWIN T. WINE LIFETIME ACHIEVEMENT
AWARD RECIPIENTS

Marilyn Rowens, The Birmingham Temple, MI – 2004

Bert W. Steinberg *, Kol Hadash, Northern CA – 2005

Rabbi Miriam S. Jerris, The Birmingham Temple, MI – 2006

Ben * & Lorraine Pivnick, The Birmingham Temple, MI – 2007

Jane Goldhamer *, Kol Shalom, OR – 2008

M. Bonnie Cousens, The Birmingham Temple, MI – 2009

Shari Gelber, Kahal B'raira, MA – 2010

Deb Godden, Machar, Washington Congregation for Secular Humanistic Judaism – 2011

Louis Altman, Kol Hadash, IL and Congregation for Humanistic Judaism, FL – 2012

Esther and Ron Milan, The Birmingham Temple, MI – 2013

Ruth Duskin Feldman *, Kol Hadash, IL – 2014

Dana and Rick Naimark, Or Adam Congregation, AZ – 2016

Larry M. Lawrence, Machar, Washington Congregation for Secular Humanistic Judaism – 2017

Andrea Friedlander, Kol Hadash Humanistic Congregation, IL – 2018

* Deceased

AFFILIATED CONGREGATIONS, COMMUNITIES, AND HAVUROT OF THE SOCIETY FOR HUMANISTIC JUDAISM

United States

ARIZONA

Or Adam Congregation for Humanistic Judaism
President Zachary Barnett, 14747 N Northsight Blvd, Suite 111-437, Scottsdale, AZ 85260, (480) 865-4710, oradaminfo@gmail.com.
www.oradam.com

Secular Humanist Jewish Circle
Catherine Becskehazy, 4994 N Louis River Way, Tucson, AZ 85718, (520) 271-4830, cathbaz@gmail.com.
www.secularhumanistjewishcircle.org

CALIFORNIA

Adat Chaverim, Congregation for Humanistic Judaism
Jonathan Friedmann, PO Box 261204, Encino, CA 91426, (888) 552-4552, info@HumanisticJudaismLA.org.
www.humanisticjudaismla.org

**Kol Hadash, Northern California
Congregation for Humanistic Judaism**
Kimberly Read, PO Box 2777, Berkeley, CA 94702, (510) 982-1455, info@kolhadash.org.
www.kolhadash.org

Pacific Community of Cultural Jews
Lee Jacobi, 23 Alameda, Irvine, CA 92620, (949) 386-0400, PacifComm@aol.com.
pccjews.org

COLORADO

Beth Ami, Colorado Congregation for Humanistic Judaism
Sheila Malcolm, 280 South 39th Street, Boulder, CO 80305,
(303) 588.0236, BethAmiInfo@gmail.com.
www.bethami.com

CONNECTICUT

Congregation for Humanistic Judaism Fairfield County
Steven Getz, PO Box 82, Westport, CT 06881,
(203) 293-8867, info@humanisticjews.org.
www.humanisticjews.org

DISTRICT OF COLUMBIA
**Machar, The Washington Congregation
for Secular Humanistic Judaism**
Rabbi Jeremy Kridel
president Joy Markowitz, PO Box 42014, Washington, D.C. 20015,
(202) 686-1881, info@machar.org.
www.machar.org

FLORIDA
Congregation Beth Adam
BJ Saul, P.O. Box 2579, Boca Raton, FL 33427
(561) 443-1769, info@bethadam.com.
www.bethadam.com

Congregation for Humanistic Judaism
Richard Stein, 3023 Proctor Road, Sarasota, FL 34231,
(941) 929-7771, CHJSarasota@hotmail.com.
www.chj-sarasota.org

ILLINOIS
Beth Chaverim Humanistic Jewish Community
Rabbi Jodi Kornfeld, Deerfield, IL 60015, (847) 945-6512,
info@bethchaverim.net.
www.bethchaverim.net

Kol Hadash Humanistic Congregation
Rabbi Adam Chalom
Susan Addelson, chair, 175 Olde Half Day Road, Suite 123,
Lincolnshire, IL 60069, (847) 383-5184, info@kolhadash.com.
www.kolhadash.com

MARYLAND

Baltimore Jewish Cultural Chavurah
Art Starr, 2 Stitchberry Court, Reisterstown, MD 21136,
(410) 493-2473, baltimoresecularjews@gmail.com.
www.baltimoresecularjews.org

MASSACHUSETTS

Kahal B'raira, Boston Congregation for Humanistic Judaism
Gladys Maged, 765 Concord Avenue, Cambridge, MA 02138,
(617) 431-3994, info@Kahalbraira.org.
www.kahalbraira.org

MICHIGAN

Birmingham Temple, Congregation for Humanistic Judaism
Rabbi Jeffrey Falick, Sherwin T. Wine z"l, Founding Rabbi
28611 W 12 Mile Road, Farmington Hills, MI 48334,
(248) 477-1410, info@birminghamtemple.org.
www.birminghamtemple.org

MINNESOTA

Or Emet, Minnesota Congregation for Humanistic Judaism
Scott Chazdon, 3116 Dean Court, Minneapolis, MN 55416,
(612) 787-7812, info@oremet.org.
www.oremet.org

NEW JERSEY

Kahal Chaverim, NJ Congregation for Humanistic Judaism
Doug Kudler, P.O. Box 238, Mt Freedom, NJ 07970,

(973) 927-0078, info@kahalchaverim.org.
www.kahalchaverim.org

NEW YORK

Beth Haskalah, Rochester Society for Humanistic Judaism
Barry Swan, P.O. Box 18343, Rochester, NY 14618-0343,
(585) 234-1644, BASWAN@aol.com.
shj-roc.org

Kol Haverim Finger Lakes Congregation for Humanistic Judaism
Abigail Cohn, PO Box 4972, Ithaca, NY 14852,
info@kolhaverim.net.
kolhaverim.net

The City Congregation for Humanistic Judaism
Rabbi Peter Schweitzer
Amy Stein, 15 West 28th Street, 3rd Floor, New York, NY 10001,
(212) 213-1002, info@citycongregation.org.
www.citycongregation.org

Westchester Community for Humanistic Judaism
Dmitry Turovsky, 84 Sprague Road, Scarsdale, NY 10583,
(914) 713-8828, info@wchj.org.
www.wchj.org

NORTH CAROLINA

Kol Haskalah, A Humanistic Jewish Congregation
Karen Schinsky, 802 Creekside Dr, Chapel Hill, NC 27516,
(919) 260-4801, info@kolhaskalah.org.
www.kolhaskalah.org/

OREGON

Kol Shalom, Community for Humanistic Judaism
DeBi Strode, 1509 SW Sunset Boulevard, Suite 1E, Portland, OR
97239, (503) 459-4210, info@kolshalom.org.
www.kolshalom.org

WASHINGTON

Secular Jewish Circle of Puget Sound
info@secularjewishcircle.org.
www.secularjewishcircle.org

Canada

ONTARIO

Oraynu Congregation
Rabbi Denise Handlarski
Roby Sadler, 156 Duncan Mill Road, Suite 14, Toronto, Ontario, M3B 3N2, Canada, (416) 385-3910, info@oraynu.org.
www.oraynu.org

SHJ@50 CELEBRATION AND SUMMIT

*At The Birmingham Temple
in Farmington Hills, Michigan
April 26-28, 2019*

May the light of Humanistic Judaism burn just as brightly for the next 50 years!

Congratulations
Myrna Baron, Founder,
& Peter Schweitzer, Rabbi Emeritus
The City Congregation, New York City

Mazal Tov to the SHJ on 50 Years

from
The International Institute
for Secular Humanistic Judaism

Training Leaders and Rabbis
Publishing Literature
Exploring Issues

of
Secular Humanistic Judaism
since 1985

WWW.IISHJ.ORG

In honor of Paul Golin
for his outstanding
leadership and vision
for SHJ

Jamie Allen Black

THE PIVNICK FAMILY FOUNDATION

Proud supporter
of Humanistic Judaism.

IN LOVING MEMORY OF PETER FRIEDMAN

SUSAN FRIEDMAN

Congratulations for Helping to Broaden the Future Shape of Judaism

Secular Humanist Jewish Circle
A Celebration of Community

Tucson, Arizona

Accolades to the SHJ@50 Planning Committee for their energy, creativity and humor on the way to the SHJ@50 celebration. L'chaim!

Mary Raskin

In honor of the Gainesville Humanistic Judaism Community, a future SHJ community

Rick Gold

In honor of Kol Shalom
for creating a community
for Humanistic Jews in
Portland, Oregon.

Mary Raskin & Gary Sampson

HUMANISTIC JUDAISM
because Secular
Jews Deserve Jewish
Community Too

Carol & Richard Logan

Congratulations
from
Kahal B'raira
with a special
shout out to
Rabbi Miriam
Jerris

Shari & Rich
Gelber

Bernard Wealth Management

Proud to be SHJ's Investment Advisor

Proud to be SHJ's Investment Advisor

HONORING
IAN ROMAN BRUSSAT
BORN
FEBRUARY 12, 2019
AND HIS PARENTS
AARON W. BRUSSAT
& ELIZABETH M.
LAWRENCE

AMY KOTKIN & LARRY
LAWRENCE

Sincere thanks to the SHJ staff
for their dedication to SHJ. Their
numerous talents, attention to
detail and resourcefulness are
significant contributions to the
SHJ@50 celebration.

Mary Raskin & Gary Sampson

"Toward the next 50
years for SHJ .... two
anonymous supporters
from Machar"

Thank you to the brilliant and dedicated volunteer leaders
who serve on the SHJ Board and throughout the
Humanistic Judaism movement. This milestone
would not have been reached without you!

With sincere appreciation,
Rabbi Miriam Jerris and Paul Golin

Mazel Tov to the SHJ
on 50 years of building
Humanistic Judaism!

Arthur Liebhaber &
Rabbi Jeffrey Falick

Mazel Tov from
Kol Hadash

Northern California Community
for Humanistic Judaism
www.kolhadash.org
Your San Francisco — Bay Area
Non-Prophet
Celebrating Cultural Judaism

Thank you to Oraynu
for providing many
opportunities to fulfill
our commitment to
tikkun olam.

Evelyn & Stanley
Goldstein

To the namesake of Miriam,
who witnessed baby Moses placed in the
Nile, and who played the timbrel and danced to
celebrate the exodus, we honor Rabbi Jerris.

Joan and Cary Shaw

Great appreciation to
Rabbi Miriam Jerris and
Madrikha Sheila Malcolm
for taking the liturgy book
from dream to reality.

Mary Raskin

Sherwin T. Wine;
For the 20th Century
Haskalah

Esther & Ron Milan

A toast to all the SHJ leaders,
past and present, who made this
anniversary celebration possible.

Andrea & Mark
Friedlander

Thank you, SHJ, for
more than thirty years
of wonderful experiences
and lasting friendships!

Faith & Steve Oremland

Mazel Tov and Yasher Koach to all Rabbis,
Madrikhim, Education and Musical
Directors, and all youth and adults who
provided meaningful leadership, enriched
our services and helped the movement
grow. And, good luck to our future leaders.

Rabbi Eva Goldfinger

Additional Support for SHJ@50

Sponsors:

Del Atwood

Darlene Basch

Ruth Bragman

Xavier & Adriel Boltaina-Bosch

Paula & Ron Creed

Jon Dickman

Christine Dunbar

Lonnie & Tom Fleischer

Jeff Friedman

David & Margo Fox

Deb & David Godden

Barbara & Donald Griss

Kol Haverim Finger Lakes Community for Humanistic Judaism

Barry Levene

Carol & Richard Logan

Machar: The Washington Congregation
for Secular Humanistic Judaism

Richard McMains

George Molnar

Dr. Jerid Morisco

Phil Padol

Deidre & Dana Preis

Joan & Michael Prival

Susan & Jim Ryan

Sheila & Ron Sebor

Herb Silverman

Marc Swetlitz

Tributes:

Eleanor Adelman

Rimma Aguirre

Patricia & Allan Becker

Beth Ami, Colorado Congregation for Humanistic Judaism

Susana & Ze'ev Brat

Kimberly Brooks

AJ & Rabbi Adam Chalom

Scott Chazdon

The City Congregation for Humanistic Judaism

Marlene Cohen

Michelle Davis

Stuart Dolnick

Stephen Evans

Ellen & Reuben Fisher

Lisa Gardner-Springer

Katherine Lato & Barry Glicklich

Gary Held

Roberta & Walter Hellman

Susan Herschman

Sandi & Robert Horwitz

Ruth Kadish

Lenore & Ron Kingston

Kol Shalom Community for Humanistic Judaism

Lauren & Dave Kopans

Robert Lasker

Jon Levine

Michael Rothschild

BJ & Rick Saul

Martin Shore

Rabbi Frank Tamburello

Terry Waslow

Rabbi Joysa Winter

Thomas Young

CPSIA information can be obtained
at www.ICGtesting.com
Printed in the USA
LVHW042331140123
736961LV00010B/1979